W9-ACP-776

THE ENCHAFÈD FLOOD

OR *The Romantic Iconography of the Sea*

These lectures were delivered at
the University of Virginia under
the Page-Barbour Foundation on
March 22, 23, 24, 1949.

The Enchafèd Flood

OR *The Romantic Iconography of the Sea*

W. H. AUDEN

RANDOM HOUSE · NEW YORK

F<small>OR</small>

ALAN ANSEN

⌇⌇⌇⌇⌇⌇⌇

*"Étude de la grande maladie de l'horreur
du domicile."*
B<small>AUDELAIRE</small>, *Mon Coeur Mis à Nu.*

ACKNOWLEDGMENT

I WISH TO EXPRESS MY THANKS to the University of Virginia and the trustees of the Page-Barbour Lecture Foundation under whose auspices the contents of this book were given in lecture form during March, 1949.

Thanks are also due to the following for the use of their translations in quotation: Kathleen Freeman (*Pre-Socratic Philosophers*), Margaret Williams (*The Wanderer and the Sea-Farer*), Alexander Dru and Walter Lowrie (Kierkegaard), Christopher Isherwood (Baudelaire's *Journals*), Helen Zimmern (Nietzsche), Helen Rootham, Norman Cameron and Delmore Schwartz (Rimbaud), Edwin Muir (Kafka).

W . H . A .

CONTENTS

ONE

The Sea and the Desert

〰〰〰〰〰

Adama: O Adam, when blew God that bitter breath
On Earth's Plain; blew He likewise on sea-deep?

Adam: I wiss not. Like to cragged desolate waste,
We lately passed, is sea-steep's haggart face.

C. M. DOUGHTY, *Adam Cast Forth*

Revolutionary changes in sensibility or style are rare. The most famous is, perhaps, the conception of *'amor'* which appeared in Europe in the twelfth century. The disappearance, during the sixteenth, of allegory as a common literary genre is another. The complex of attitudes and styles which emerges towards the end of the eighteenth century and is called, more conveniently than accurately, Romanticism is a third.

These chapters are an attempt to understand the nature of Romanticism through an examination of its treatment of a single theme, the sea.

*

Near the beginning of the fifth book of *The Prelude*, Wordsworth describes in some detail a dream. It is, perhaps, an indication that, to him, this dream was of particular importance, that the 1805 and the 1850 versions differ. In the first it is assigned to a friend, in the second to Wordsworth himself. This is the 1805 text.

. . . once upon a summer's noon,
While he was sitting in a rocky cave
By the sea-side, perusing, as it chanced,
The famous History of the Errant Knight
Recorded by Cervantes, these same thoughts
Came to him; and to height unusual rose
While listlessly he sate, and having closed
The Book, had turned his eyes towards the Sea.
On Poetry and geometric Truth,
The knowledge that endures, upon these two,
And their high privilege of lasting life,
Exempt from all internal injury,
He mused: upon these chiefly: and at length,
His senses yielding to the sultry air,
Sleep seiz'd him, and he pass'd into a dream.
He saw before him an Arabian Waste,
A Desart; and he fancied that himself
Was sitting there in the wide wilderness,
Alone, upon the sands. Distress of mind
Was growing in him, when, behold! at once
To his great joy a Man was at his side,
Upon a dromedary, mounted high.
He seem'd an Arab of the Bedouin Tribes,
A lance he bore, and underneath one arm
A Stone; and, in the opposite hand, a Shell
Of a surpassing brightness. Much rejoic'd
The dreaming Man that he should have a Guide
To lead him through the Desart; and he thought,
While questioning himself what this strange freight
Which the Newcomer carried through the Waste
Could mean, the Arab told him that the Stone,
To give it in the language of the Dream,

Was Euclid's Elements; 'and this,' said he,
'This other,' pointing to the Shell, 'this Book
Is something of more worth.' And, at the word,
The Stranger, said my Friend continuing,
Stretch'd forth the Shell towards me, with command
That I should hold it to my ear; I did so,
And heard that instant in an unknown Tongue,
Which yet I understood, articulate sounds,
A loud prophetic blast of harmony,
An Ode, in passion utter'd, which foretold
Destruction to the Children of the Earth,
By deluge now at hand. No sooner ceas'd
The Song, but with calm look, the Arab said
That all was true; that it was even so
As had been spoken; and that he himself
Was going then to bury those two Books:
The one that held acquaintance with the stars,
And wedded man to man by purest bond
Of nature, undisturbed by space or time;
Th' other that was a God, yea many Gods,
Had voices more than all the winds, and was
A joy, a consolation, and a hope.
My friend continued, 'strange as it may seem,
I wonder'd not, although I plainly saw
The one to be a Stone, th' other a Shell,
Nor doubted once but that they both were Books,
Having a perfect faith in all that pass'd
A wish was now ingender'd in my fear
To cleave unto this Man, and I begg'd leave
To share his errand with him. On he pass'd
Not heeding me; I follow'd, and took note
That he look'd often backward with wild look,

Grasping his twofold treasure to his side.
—Upon a Dromedary, Lance in rest,
He rode, I keeping pace with him, and now
I fancied that he was the very Knight
Whose Tale Cervantes tells, yet not the Knight,
But was an Arab of the Desert, too;
Of these was neither, and was both at once.
His countenance, meanwhile, grew more disturb'd.
And looking backwards when he look'd, I saw
A glittering light, and ask'd him whence it came.
'It is,' said he, 'the waters of the deep
Gathering upon us,' quickening then his pace
He left me: I call'd after him aloud;
He heeded not; but with his twofold charge
Beneath his arm, before me full in view
I saw him riding o'er the Desert Sands,
With the fleet waters of the drowning world
In chase of him, whereat I wak'd in terror,
And saw the Sea before me; and the Book,
In which I had been reading, at my side.'

Book V. 56–139

Here are three pairs of symbols:

1) The desert and the sea
2) The stone of abstract geometry, and the shell of imagination or instinct, which between them offer alternative routes of salvation from the anxiety of the dreamer, a promise which is not realised.
3) The double-natured hero, half Bedouin, i.e., Ishmael, the exile, the Wandering Jew, the Flying Dutchman, and half Don Quixote, i.e., the dedicated man, the Knight of Faith who would restore the Age of Gold.

THE SEA

The second verse of the first chapter of the Book of Genesis runs as follows:

And the earth was without form, and void; and darkness was upon the face of the deep. And the Spirit of God moved upon the face of the waters.

On the first day God said, Let there be light, on the second He

made the firmament, and divided the waters which were under the firmament from the waters which were above the firmament.

And on the third He gathered the waters under the heaven

unto one place, and let the dry land appear; and the gathering together of the waters called he Seas.

Similarly in one of the Greek cosmologies, the beginning of everything was when Eros issued from the egg of Night which floated upon Chaos.

The sea or the great waters, that is, are the symbol for the primordial undifferentiated flux, the substance which became created nature only by having form imposed upon or wedded to it.

The sea, in fact, is that state of barbaric vagueness and disorder out of which civilisation has emerged and into which, unless saved by the effort of gods and men, it is always liable to relapse. It is so little of a friendly symbol that the first thing which the author of the

7

Book of Revelation notices in his vision of the new heaven and earth at the end of time is that *'there was no more sea.'*

In consequence, though the metaphor of the ship of state or society appears early, it is only employed when society is in peril. The ship ought not to be out of harbor. Thus Horace writes

> *O navis, referent in mare te novi*
> *fluctus. O quid agis! fortiter occupa*
> > *portum.*

O ship, new billows are carrying you out to sea. What are you doing? Struggle to reach port.

(Odes I.14)

The ship, then, is only used as a metaphor for society in danger from within or without. When society is normal the image is the City or the Garden. That is where people want and ought to be. As to the sea, the classical authors would have agreed with Marianne Moore. "It is human nature to stand in the middle of a thing; But you cannot stand in the middle of this." A voyage, therefore, is a necessary evil, a crossing of that which separates or estranges. Neither Odysseus nor Jason goes to sea for the sake of the voyage; the former is trying to get home and, if it were not for the enmity of Poseidon, the father of the monster Cyclops, it would be soon over, which is what Odysseus most desires; the latter is trying to capture the Golden Fleece, which is in a distant country, to bring back to his own. If it were nearer and no voyage were necessary, he would be much relieved.*

The state ship that deliberately chooses the high seas is the state in disorder, the Ship of Fools, as in Barclay's adaptation of Brant's *Narrenschiff:*

> Lyke as a myrrour doth represent agayne
> The fourme and fygure of mannes countenaunce
> So in our ship shall he se wrytyn playne
> The fourme and fygure of hys mysgovernaunce.

"What ship is that with so many owners and strange tackle? It is a great vessel. This is the ship of Fools where saileth both spiritual and temporal of every calling some. This ship wanteth a good pilot, the storm, the rocks and the wrecks at hand; all must come to naught for want of good government." †

---

* The Christian conception of time as a divine creation, to be accepted, and not, as in Platonic and Stoic philosophy, ignored, made the journey or pilgrimage a natural symbol for the spiritual life. Similarly the injunction "Whosoever will come after me, let him deny himself, and take up his cross, and follow me" and the distinction between the Kingdom of Heaven and the Kingdom of this world contradicts the classical hope of the perfect *polis*. But, so far as I know, the pilgrimage of the pious soul is never symbolised in early Christian literature by a sea-voyage.

† This looks so similar to the behaviour of the Jumblies, but how differently the reader is expected to feel towards the latter.

> They went to sea in a sieve, they did.
> In a sieve they went to sea:
> In spite of all their friends could say
> On a winter's morn, on a stormy day
> In a sieve they went to sea!
> And when the sieve turned round and round
> And everyone cried, "You'll all be drowned!"
> They called aloud, "Our sieve ain't big,
> But we don't care a button! we don't care a fig!
> In a sieve we'll go to sea."

Similarly in the Anglo-Saxon poems, *The Wanderer* and *The Seafarer*, the mariner is to be pitied rather than admired, for he

>   heart weary
> Over ocean streams must for long
> Stir with hands   frost-cold sea
> Rove paths of exile.
>
>   No protecting kinsman
> Can bring comfort to the soul in loneliness.
> Full little he thinks who has life's joy
> And dwells in cities and has few disasters,
> Proud and wine-flushed, how I, weary often,
> Must bide my time on the brimming stream.

The sea is no place to be if you can help it, and to try to cross it betrays a rashness bordering on hubris, at which a man's friends should be properly concerned.

> *Nequiquam deus abscidit*
>   *prudens Oceano dissociabile*
> *terras si tamen impiae*
>   *non tangenda rates transiliunt vada.*

Vain was the purpose of the god in severing the lands by the estranging sea, if in spite of him our impious ships dash across the depths he meant should never be touched.

(Horace Odes I. 3)

There is a famous passage in the 26th canto of Dante's *Inferno* which is interesting not only for its beauty, but because the legend of Ulysses' last voyage appears to be Dante's own invention.

Ulysses is in Hell for having been an Evil Counsellor. Dante begins rather mysteriously

I sorrowed then, and sorrow now again when I direct my memory to what I saw; and curb my genius more than I am wont lest it run where Virtue guides it not.

Ulysses in describing his end says: "Neither fondness for my son nor reverence for my aged father, nor the due love that should have cheered Penelope could conquer in me the ardor that I had to gain experience of the world, of human vice and worth." To his fellow-mariners he had argued: "Consider your origin: ye were not formed to live like brutes but to follow virtue and knowledge."

Ulysses behaves like the typical Romantic Marine Hero, which in Tennyson's version of the same story he, indeed, becomes, but to Dante, clearly, his action was not only reprehensible but, as the last sentence shows, essentially the original sin of Adam, and in his speech to his fellows, he is once more, as earlier at Troy, the Evil Counsellor whose words echo the words of the Serpent to Eve. Perhaps, too, Dante's opening remarks indicate that the same temptation to the concupiscence of curiosity was his own.

The handling of the symbols of sea and storm by Shakespeare provides us with a bridge between what, for convenience, one may call the classic attitude and the romantic. The subject has been so exhaustively and sensitively studied by Mr. Wilson Knight in *The Shakesperian Tempest* * as to make much further comment superfluous. As Wilson Knight demonstrates, in most of Shakespeare's plays there are two antithetical symbolic clusters. On the one hand tempests, rough beasts, comets, diseases, malice domestic and private vice, that is, the world of conflict and disorder; on the other hand music, flowers, birds, precious stones and marriage, the world of reconciliation and order. In the earlier plays the stormy sea is more purely negative, a reflection of human conflict or the fatal mischance which provides evil with its opportunity (e.g. *Othello*). In the last plays, *Pericles, The Winter's Tale, The Tempest*, however, not only do the sea and the sea voyage play a much more important role, but also a different one. The sea becomes the place of purgatorial suffering: through separation and apparent loss, the characters disordered by passion are brought to their senses and the world of music and marriage is made possible. There is, however, one extremely important difference in the relation of the actors to the sea from that which our period exhibits, namely, that the putting to sea, the wandering is never *voluntarily* entered upon as a pleasure. It is a pain which must be accepted as cure, the death that leads to rebirth, in order that the abiding city may be built. Deliberately to seek the exile is still folly. Thus, in *The Winter's Tale* the good old counsellor Camillo advises the young lovers

---

* Oxford Press, 1932

Florizel and Perdita to enlist the help of Leontes rather than to elope.

> A course more promising
> Than a wild dedication of yourselves
> To unpath'd waters, undream'd shores, most certain
> To miseries enough: no hope to help you,
> But as you shake off one to take another;
> Nothing so certain as your anchors, who
> Do their best office, if they can but stay you
> Where you'll be loath to be.
>
> *The Winter's Tale* iv 4

The distinctive new notes in the Romantic attitude are as follows.
1) To leave the land and the city is the desire of every man of sensibility and honor.
2) The sea is the real situation and the voyage is the true condition of man.

"The port we sail from is far astern and, though far out of sight of land, for ages and ages we continue to sail with sealed orders and our last destination remains a secret to ourselves and our officers. And yet our final haven was predestined ere we stepped from the stocks of creation. Let us not give ear to the superstitious gun-deck gossip about whither we may be gliding for, as yet, not a soul on board of us knows—not even the commodore himself—assuredly not the chaplain—even our professors' scientific surmisings are vain. On that point, the smallest cabin boy is as wise as the captain."

(White Jacket)

13

3) The sea is where the decisive events, the moments of eternal choice, of temptation, fall, and redemption occur. The shore life is always trivial.

4) An abiding destination is unknown even if it may exist: a lasting relationship is not possible nor even to be desired.

> *Les vrais voyageurs sont ceux-là seuls qui partent*
> *Pour partir; coeurs légers, semblables aux ballons,*
> *De leur fatalité jamais ils ne s'écartent,*
> *Et, sans savoir pourquoi, disent toujours: Allons!*
> Baudelaire (*Le Voyage*)

THE DESERT

Like the sea, the desert is the nucleus of a cluster of traditional associations.

1) It is the place where the water of life is lacking, the valley of dry bones in Ezekiel's vision.

2) It may be so by nature, i.e., the wilderness which lies *outside* the fertile place or city. As such, it is the place where nobody desires by nature to be. Either one is compelled by others to go there because one is a criminal outlaw or a scapegoat (e.g. Cain, Ishmael), or one chooses to withdraw from the city in order to be alone. This withdrawal may be temporary, a period of self-examination and purification in order to return to the city with a true knowledge of one's mission and the strength to carry it out (e.g. Jesus' forty days in the wilderness), or it may be permanent, a final rejection of the wicked

city of this world, a dying to the life of the flesh and an assumption of a life devoted wholly to spiritual contemplation and prayer (e.g. the Thebaid).

3) The natural desert is therefore at once the place of punishment for those rejected by the good city because they are evil, and the place of purgation for those who reject the evil city because they desire to become good. In the first case the desert image is primarily related to the idea of justice, i.e., the desert is the place outside the law. As such it may be the home of the dragon or any lawless power which is hostile to the city and so be the place out into which the hero must venture in order to deliver the city from danger. An elaboration of this is the myth of the treasure in the desert guarded by the dragon. This treasure belongs by right to the city and has either been stolen by force or lost through the city's own sin. The hero then performs a double task. He delivers the city from danger and restores the precious life-giving object to its rightful owners.

In the second case, when the desert is the purgative place, the image is primarily associated with the idea of chastity and humility. It is the place where there are no beautiful bodies or comfortable beds or stimulating food and drink or admiration. The temptations of the desert are therefore either sexual mirages raised by the devil to make the hermit nostalgic for his old life or the more subtle temptations of pride when the devil appears in his own form.

4) The natural wilderness may lie not only outside the city but also *between* one city and another, i.e., be the place to be crossed, in which case the image is associated with the idea of vocation. Only the individual or community with the faith and courage which can dare, endure, and survive its trials is worthy to enter into the promised land of the New Life.

5) Lastly, the desert may not be barren by nature but as the consequence of a historical catastrophe. The once-fertile city has become, through the malevolence of others or its own sin, the waste land. In this case it is the opportunity for the stranger hero who comes from elsewhere to discover the cause of the disaster, destroy or heal it and become the rebuilder of the city and, in most cases, its new ruler.

THE ROMANTIC SEA AND THE ROMANTIC DESERT

Resemblances

1) Both are the wilderness, i.e., the place where there is no community, just or unjust, and no historical change for better or for worse.

2) Therefore the individual in either is free from both the evils and the responsibilities of communal life. Thus Byron writes of the ocean:

> Man marks the earth with ruin—his control
> Stops with the shore.
>
> (*Childe Harold*)

And Captain Nemo, the commander of the submarine *Nautilus* in *Twenty Thousand Leagues Under the Sea*, cries:

"The sea does not belong to despots. Upon its surface men can still exercise unjust laws, fight, tear one another to pieces, and be carried away with terrestrial horrors. But at thirty feet below its level, their reign ceases, their influence is quenched, and their power disappears. Ah, sir; live, live in the bosom of the waters. There only is independence. There I recognize no master's voice. There I am free."

And so Carmen tempts Don José to leave the fertile plain for the barren lawless mountains.

> *Tu n'y dépendrais de personne.*
> *Point d'officier à qui tu doives obéir*
> *Et point de retraite qui sonne*
> *Pour dire à l'amoureux qu'il est temps de partir.*

Both, in fact, are characterised by the absence of limitations, of '*les arrêts de la vie*,' the Ocean-chart that the Bellman bought describes them well.

"What's the good of Mercator's North Poles and Equators,
  Tropics, Zones, and Meridian Lines?"
So the Bellman would cry: and the crew would reply
  "They are merely conventional signs!

"Other maps are such shapes, with their islands and capes!
  But we've got our brave Captain to thank"
(So the crew would protest) "that he's bought *us* the best—
  A perfect and absolute blank!"

17

Le ciel ouvert
La vie errante
Pour pays l'univers
Et pour loi sa volonté
Et surtout la chose enivrante
La liberté.

Meilhac and Halévy (*Carmen*)

3) But precisely because they are free places, they are
also lonely places of alienation, and the individual
who finds himself there, whether by choice or fate,
must from time to time, rightly or wrongly, be visited
by desperate longings for home and company. So
Ishmael, however he may convince himself that "in
landlessness alone resides highest truth, shoreless,
indefinite as God—so better is it to perish in that
lonely infinite than be ingloriously dashed upon the
lea, even if that were safety," nevertheless, as he
squeezes out the whale sperm with his hands, he is
compelled to reflect that "Happiness is not in the
intellect or the fancy—but in the wife, the heart, the
bed, the table, the saddle, the fireside, the country."
So Ahab, on that final beautiful day before his encounter with Moby Dick, softens and calls despair-
ingly to Starbuck: "Stand close to me, Starbuck; let
me look into a human eye; it is better than to gaze
into sea or sky; better than to gaze upon God. By
the green land; by the bright hearthstone! this is the
magic glass, man; I see my wife and my child in
thine eye. . . . It is a mild, mild wind, and a mild-
looking meadow; they have been making hay some-

where under the slopes of the Andes, Starbuck, and the mowers are sleeping among the new-mown hay." Even that most passionate Don Quixote of absolute freedom, the Rimbaud of *Bateau Ivre*, is forced to confess

> *Je regrette l'Europe aux anciens parapets*

and to remember nostalgically a time of a more restricted loneliness when on a black cold pond

> *Un enfant accroupi, plein de tristesse, lâche*
> *Un bateau frêle comme un papillon de mai.*

And so too in his moment of greatest anguish when the Ancient Mariner is

> Alone, alone, all, all alone
> Alone on a wide wide sea!

he looks up yearningly to the moon and the stars and the blue sky which, says the Gloss, "belongs to them, and is their appointed rest, and their native country and their own natural homes." And when he repents, and the ship begins to move again, he is refreshed by the sound of the sails

> A noise like of a hidden brook
> In the leafy month of June,
> That to the sleeping woods all night
> Singeth a quiet tune.

Differences

As places of freedom and solitude the sea and the desert are symbolically the same. In other respects, however, they are opposites. E.g. the desert is the dried-up place, i.e., the place where life has ended, the Omega of temporal existence. Its first most obvious characteristic is that nothing moves; the second is that everything is surface and exposed. No soil, no hidden spring. The sea, on the other hand, is the Alpha of existence, the symbol of potentiality.

> Thy shores are empires, changed in all save thee—
> Assyria, Greece, Rome, Carthage, what are they?
> Thy waters wash'd them power while they were free,
> And many a tyrant since; their shores obey
> The stranger, slave, or savage; their decay
> Has dried up realms to deserts:—not so thou;—
> Unchangeable, save to thy wild waves' play,
> Time notes no wrinkle on thine azure brow:
> Such as creation's dawn beheld, thou rollest now.
>   (*Childe Harold* Canto IV)

Its first most obvious characteristic is its perpetual motion, the violence of wave as tempest; its power may be destructive, but unlike that of the desert, it is positive. Its second is the teeming life that lies hidden below the surface which, however dreadful, is greater than the visible: "As this appalling ocean surrounds the verdant land, so in the soul of man there lies one insular Tahiti, full of peace and joy, but encompassed by all the horror of the half-known life."(*Moby Dick*)

The sea, then, is the symbol of primitive potential power as contrasted with the desert of actualised triviality, of living barbarism versus lifeless decadence.

THE OASIS AND THE HAPPY ISLAND

The sea and the desert are related to the city as its symbolic opposites. There is a third image, in the case of the sea the happy island and in the case of the desert the oasis or rose garden, which stands related to both. It is like the city in that it is an enclosed place of safety and like the sea-desert in that it is a solitary or private place from which the general public are excluded and where the writ of the law does not run. The primary idea with which the garden-island image is associated is, therefore, neither justice nor chastity but innocence; it is the earthly paradise where there is no conflict between natural desire and moral duty.

Thus Pindar sings in the second Olympian of the land of the Hyperboreans

> In sunshine ever fair
> Abide the Good and all their nights and days
> An equal splendour wear.
> And never as of old with thankless toil
> For their poor empty needs they vex the soil
> And plough the watery seas
> But dwelling with the glorious gods in ease
> A tearless life they pass.

And Euripides in *Hippolytus*

> To the strand of the Daughters of the sunset,
> The apple tree, the singing and the gold;
> Where the mariner must stay him from his onset
> And the red wave is tranquil as of old;
> Yea beyond that Pillar of the End
> That Atlas guardeth, would I wend.

21

And the same nostalgia is common among the romantics, for *l'innocent paradis, plein de plaisirs furtifs,* where

> *tout n'est qu'ordre et beauté*
> *Luxe, calme et volupté.*

This image, in its turn, has two possibilities. Either it is the real earthly paradise, in which case it is a place of temporary refreshment for the exhausted hero, a foretaste of rewards to come or the final goal and reward itself, where the beloved and the blessed society are waiting to receive him into their select company; or it is a magical garden, an illusion caused by black magic to tempt the hero to abandon his quest, and which, when the spell is broken, is seen to be really the desert of barren rock, or a place of horror like Calypso's island, Klingsor's garden, or the isle of Venus.*

---

* An interesting example of the tempting island imagery because of the unusual twist given to it is Tennyson's *Voyage of Maeldune.* In this poem there are nine islands which I associate, perhaps rather arbitrarily, with certain ideas as follows.

The Silent Isle	Introversion
The Shouting Isle	Extroversion
The Isle of Flowers but no Fruits	Art
The Isle of Fruits	Science
The Isle of Fire	Materialism
The Isle under the Sea	Mysticism
The Beauteous Isle	Leisure
The Isle of Witches	Sex
The Isle of Double Towers	Religious and Political Fanaticism

Maeldune's crew, when they first sight these islands, expect to enjoy themselves, i.e., they expect to be tempted to stay and be untrue to

THE ROMANTIC OASIS-ISLAND

The image of the happy Prelapsarian Place appears often enough in Romantic literature but charged usually with a hopeless nostalgia. The examples which the romantic actually encounters turn out to be mirages or disappointing and dangerous deserts like the *Encantadas* of which Melville writes:

"Change never comes, neither the change of seasons nor of sorrows. No voice, no low, no howl is heard: the chief sound of life here is a hiss. In no world but a fallen one could such lands exist."

Where the population consists of

Mcn	0
Ant-eaters	Unknown
Man-haters	Unknown
Lizards	500,000
Snakes	500,000
Spiders	10,000,000
Salamanders	Unknown
Devils	Do. Do.

Eldorado turns out to be a reef, the island of Cythera is

un terrain des plus maigres,
Un désert rocailleux troublé par des cris aigres
Baudelaire (*Voyage à Cythère*)

---

their mission, which is one of vengeance. What happens, however, is that the islands turn out to be places of danger which make them kill each other or commit suicide, i.e., turn their aggressive feelings away from the absent object against themselves. Thus the islands become the means by which Maeldune and they are taught through suffering from hate that hate is hateful.

When at last they landed on the shore where the Snarks were to be found

> the crew were not pleased with the view
> Which consisted of chasms and crags.

And the natural surroundings of Lady Jingly Jones are in keeping with her lovelorn condition

> On that coast of Coromandel
> In his jug without a handle
> Still she weeps and still she moans,
> On that little heap of stones.

The tempestuous liquid sea is dangerous enough but when it approaches the condition of the solid desert it is worse. E.g. the sand-bank of the Kentish Knock in *The Wreck of the Deutschland* and the iceberg in Melville's poem

> Hard Berg (methought), so cold, so vast,
> With mortal damps self-overcast;
> Exhaling still thy dankish breath—
> Adrift dissolving, bound for death;
> Though lumpish thou, a lumbering one—
> A lumbering lubbard loitering slow,
> Impingers rue thee and go down
> Sounding thy precipice below,
> Nor stir the slimy slug that sprawls
> Along thy dead indifference of walls.

And the Ancient Mariner's punishment begins when the sea becomes a counterfeit desert.

> Day after day, day after day,
> We stuck, nor breath nor motion;
> As idle as a painted ship
> Upon a painted ocean.
>
> Water, water, everywhere,
> And all the boards did shrink;
> Water, water, everywhere,
> Nor any drop to drink.
>
> The very deep did rot: O Christ!
> That ever this should be!
> Yea, slimy things did crawl with legs
> Upon the slimy sea.

To the romantic, that is, childhood is over, its island is astern, and there is no other. The only possible place of peace now lies under the waters.

"Where lies the final harbor whence we unmoor no more? Where is the foundling's father hidden? Our souls are like those orphans whose unwedded mothers die in bearing them: the secret of our paternity lies in their grave, and we must there to learn it."

(*Moby Dick*)

The images of the Just City, of the civilised landscape protected by the Madonna, the "*Fior, frondi, ombre,*

25

antri, onde, aure soavi" which look at us from so many Italian paintings, and of the rose garden or island of the blessed, are lacking in Romantic literature because the Romantic writers no longer believe in their existence. What exists is the Trivial Unhappy Unjust City, the desert of the average from which the only escape is to the wild, lonely, but still vital sea. The Desert has become, in fact, an image of modern civilisation in which innocence and the individual are alike destroyed.

THE LEVEL DESERT

None of the writers we are discussing had much good to say for laissez-faire democracy. Rimbaud's poem on that subject expresses an attitude shared by most of them.

DEMOCRACY

The flag is in keeping with the unclean landscape, and our jargon drowns the sound of the drums.

At certain centres we will encourage the most cynical prostitution. We will crush logical rebellion.

Let us go to dusty and exhausted countries—put ourselves at the service of monstrous industrial or military exploitations.

"To our next meeting—here—no matter where!"

Conscripts of good intentions we shall have a ferocious philosophy. Dunces shall be devotees of knowledge, sybarites enthusiasts for comfort; and for this busy world there shall be dissolution.

This is real progress! Forward! March!

(Les Illuminations)

And Baudelaire foresaw a democratic future when "the son will run away from the family not at eighteen but at twelve, emancipated by his gluttonous precocity; he will fly, not to seek heroic adventures, not to deliver a beautiful prisoner from a tower, not to immortalize a garret with sublime thoughts, but to found a business, to enrich himself and to compete with his infamous papa" and the daughter, "with an infantile wantonness, will dream in her cradle that she sells herself for a million."

(Fusées)

They did not feel like this because they disbelieved in individual freedom but precisely because, passionately believing in it, they saw urban democracy as they knew it, destroying the heroic individual and turning him into a cypher of the crowd, or a mechanical cogwheel in an impersonal machine.

What Baudelaire stigmatises as *l'esprit belge*, what Jack Chase means when he says, "let us hate the public and cleave to the people," what Lear means by They in such a limerick as

> There was an old man of Whitehaven
> Who danced a quadrille with a raven

> They said: It's absurd
> To encourage this bird
> So they smashed that old man of Whitehaven.

is dealt with most fully by Kierkegaard:

> "The man who has no opinion of an event at the actual
> moment accepts the opinion of the majority, or if he is quar-
> relsome, of the minority. But it must be remembered that
> both majority and minority are real people, and that is why
> the individual is assisted by adhering to them. A public, on
> the contrary, is an abstraction . . . A public is neither a
> nation, nor a generation, nor a community, nor these par-
> ticular men, for all these are only what they are through the
> concrete; no single person who belongs to the public makes a
> real commitment; for some hours of the day, perhaps, he
> belongs to the public—at moments when he is nothing else,
> since when he is really what he is he does not form part of the
> public. Made up of such individuals, of individuals at the
> moments when they are nothing, a public is a kind of gigantic
> something, an abstract and deserted void which is everything
> and nothing."

> *(Thoughts on the Present Age)*

So, too, Wordsworth saw the London crowds:

> The slaves unrespited of low pursuits,
> Living amid the same perpetual flow
> Of trivial objects, melted and reduced
> To one identity, by differences
> That have no law, no meaning, and no end.
> *(Prelude* VII 700–704)

Again, although it has struck many readers as unjust, Coleridge was imaginatively correct in allowing all the companions of the Ancient Mariner to die. The latter has sinned by shooting the Albatross, but the sin is a personal act for which he can suffer and repent. The rest of the crew react collectively as a crowd, not as persons. First they blame him because they think he has killed the bird that made the breeze to blow, then they praise him for having killed the bird that brought the fog and mist, and then when the ship is becalmed, they turn on him again and hang the albatross around his neck. That is to say, they are an irresponsible crowd and since, as such, they can take no part in the Mariner's personal repentance, they must die to be got out of the way.

THE MECHANISED DESERT

If, in the overlarge, industrialised cities against which the romantic poets protest, the masses during their hours of leisure lack any real common bond of love or commitment and turn into crowds, in their working hours they tend to become mere instruments of their particular function, to have no existence over and above what they do to earn their living.

With the exception of the Beaver, the Bellman's crew in *The Hunting of the Snark* have no names, only jobs, Boots, Maker of Bonnets and Hoods, Barrister, Broker, Billiard Marker, Banker, Butcher, and Baker (the reason why the last is said to have forgotten his name, we shall consider later). It is not that they are passionate about these jobs, dedicated to them by a personal choice, no, these are just what they happen to do. The best portrait of this depersonalised technician is the Carpenter of the *Pequod*, "a strict abstract" who "works by a deaf and dumb spontaneous literal process, a pure manipulator: his brain, if he had ever had one, must have early oozed along with the muscles of his fingers." He is a solitary who has no relationships with human beings, only with wood and his tools, without being a simple individual. Then he continually talks to himself, but is incapable of a real dialogue of self with self, only a meaningless stream of free associations set off by the actions of his fingers, soliloquising "like the whirring wheel—to keep himself awake."

Drat the file, and drat the bone! That is hard which should be soft, and that is soft which should be hard. So we go, who file old jaws and shinbones. Let's try another. Aye, now, this works better (*sneezes*). Halloa, this bone dust is (*sneezes*)— why it's (*sneezes*)—yes, it's (*sneezes*)—bless my soul, it won't let me speak! This is what an old fellow gets now for working in dead lumber. Saw a live tree, and you don't get this dust; amputate a live bone, and you don't get it (*sneezes*). Come, come, you old Smut, there, bear a hand, and let's have that ferule and buckle-screw; I'll be ready for them presently. Lucky now (*sneezes*) there's no knee-joint to make; that might puzzle a little; but a mere shinbone—why it's easy as making hop-poles; only I should like to put a good finish on. Time, time; if I but only had the time, I could turn him out as neat a leg now as ever scraped to a lady in a parlor . . . There!

before I saw it off, now, I must call his old Mogulship, and see
whether the length will be all right; too short, if anything, I
guess. Ha! that's the heel; we are in luck; here he comes,
or it's somebody else, that's certain.

(*Moby Dick*. Chapter cviii)

What has happened, in fact, is the disappearance of a
true community, i.e., a group of rational beings associated on the basis of a common love. Societies still exist,
i.e., organisations of talents for the sake of a given function. Communities and societies are not identical, i.e.,
a cello player in a string quartet, who hates music but
plays because he must eat and playing the cello is all
he knows, is a member of a society; he is not a member
of the community of music lovers, but in a healthy
culture societies exist as differentiated units inside a
common community.

In a society, where the structure and relation of its
members to each other is determined by the function
for which the society exists and not by their personal
choice, the whole is more real than the sum of its parts.
In a community, on the other hand, which is determined by the subjective verbs Love or Believe, *I* always
precedes *We*. In a closed traditional community this
fact is hidden, because the *I* is only potential. The be-
liever by tradition is unconscious of any alternative to
his belief—he has only heard of one kind of snark, and
therefore cannot doubt. The further civilisation moves
towards the open condition in which each man is conscious that there are snarks that have feathers and bite

and snarks that have whiskers and scratch, the sharper becomes the alternative: *either* personal choice and through the sum of such choices an actual community *or* the annihilation of personality and the dissolution of community into crowds.

A cartoon by Charles Addams which appeared some years ago in *The New Yorker* illustrates admirably the urban situation in which individuality is lost. It shows a residential street in New York. Along the pavement a motionless line of spectators is staring at a little man with an umbrella engaged in a life-and-death struggle with a large octopus which has emerged from a manhole in the middle of the street. Behind the crowd two men with brief-cases are walking along without bothering to turn their heads and one is saying to the other: "It doesn't take much to collect a crowd in New York."

The cartoon contains three groups:

1) The majority crowd, no member of which dares move unless the rest do so, so that all remain passive spectators and not one steps out to help the man in trouble and, by doing so, to become an individual.

2) The minority crowd who are, indeed, acting (they are walking, not standing still) but whose actions and feelings are negatively conditioned by the majority, i.e., what they do is not their personal choice, but whatever it may be that the majority does *not* do.

3) The single man struggling with the octopus. He is a real individual, yet even with him, the question arises: "Would he be standing out there in the street

by himself if the octopus had not attacked him?"
i.e., if he had not been compelled by a fate outside
his personal control to become the exceptional individual. There is even a suggestion about his bourgeois umbrella of a magician's wand. Could it be
possible that, desiring to become an individual yet
unable to do so by himself, he has conjured up a
monster from the depths of the sea to break the
spell of reflection, and free him from being just a
member of the crowd?

It is not only the little man in the bowler hat, however, who is in danger of loss of individuality. As
Nietzsche perceived, the brilliant scholarly mind is, in
modern civilisation, even more threatened.

However gratefully one may welcome the objective spirit—
and who has not been sick to death of all subjectivity and its
confounded *ipsisimosity*—in the end, however, one must learn
caution, even with regard to one's gratitude, and put a stop
to the exaggeration with which the unselfing and depeson-
alising of the spirit has recently been celebrated, as if it were
the goal in itself, as if it were a salvation and glorification—
as is especially accustomed to happen in the pessimist school,
which has also in its turn good reasons for paying the highest
honours to "disinterested knowledge." The objective man,
who no longer curses and scolds like the pessimist, the *ideal*
man of learning in whom the scientific instinct blossoms forth
fully after a thousand complete and partial failures, is surely
one of the most costly instruments that exist, but his place is
in the hand of one who is more powerful. He is only an instru-
ment—we may say he is a *mirror*, he is no "purpose in him-

self." The objective man is in truth a mirror. Accustomed to prostration before everything that wants to be known, with such desires only as knowing and reflecting imply—he waits until something comes, and then expands himself sensitively, so that even the lightest footsteps and gliding past of spiritual beings may not be lost on his surface and film. Whatever "personality" he still possesses seems to him accidental, arbitrary, or still oftener disturbing; so much has he come to regard himself as the passage and reflection of outside forms and events. He calls up the recollection of "himself" with an effort. He readily confounds himself with other people, he makes mistakes with regard to his own needs, and here only is he unrefined and negligent. Perhaps he is troubled about the health, or the pettiness and confined atmosphere of wife and friend, or the lack of companions and society—and indeed, he sets himself to reflect on his suffering, but in vain! His thoughts already rove away to the *more general* case, and tomorrow he knows as little as he knew yesterday how to help himself. He does not now take himself seriously and devote time to himself: he is serene, *not* from lack of troubles, but from lack of capacity for grasping and dealing with *his* trouble. The habitual complaisance with respect to all objects and experiences, the radiant and impartial hospitality with which he receives everything that comes his way, his habit of inconsiderate good nature, of dangerous indifference to Yea and Nay . . . Should one wish Love or Hatred from him— and I mean Love and Hatred as God, woman and animal understand them, he will do what he can, and furnish what he can. But one must not be surprised if it should not be much— if he should show himself just at this point to be false, fragile, and rather *un tour de force*, a slight ostentation and exaggeration. He is only genuine so far as he can be objective;

only in his serene totality is he still "nature" and "natural." His mirroring and eternally self-polishing soul no longer knows how to affirm, no longer how to deny; he does not command; neither does he destroy. "Je ne méprise presque rien"—he says with Leibnitz: let us not overlook nor undervalue the *presque!*

(*Beyond Good and Evil*)

If a community so dissolves, the societies, which remain so long as human beings wish to remain alive, must, left to themselves, grow more and more mechanical. And such real individuals as are left must become Ishmaels, "isolatoes, not acknowledging the common continent of men, but each isolatoe living in a separate continent of his own;" Hamlet is at the mercy of reflection and melancholia.

What it feels like to be such an isolatoe, who cannot take the crowd way and become a grain of the desert sand, but is left standing there alone in the wide waste, is described similarly by most of them.

Thus Coleridge:

> A grief without a pang, void, dark, and drear,
>   A stifled, drowsy, unimpassioned grief,
>   Which finds no natural outlet, no relief,
>   In word, or sigh, or tear—
> O Lady! in this wan and heartless mood,
> To other thoughts by yonder throstle wooed,
>   All this long eve, so balmy and serene,
> Have I been gazing on the western sky,
>   And its peculiar tint of yellow green:
> And still I gaze—and with how blank an eye!

And those thin clouds above, in flakes and bars,
That give away their motion to the stars;
Those stars, that glide behind them or between,
Now sparkling, now bedimmed, but always seen:
Yon crescent Moon, as fixed as if it grew
In its own cloudless, starless lake of blue,
I see them all so excellently fair,
I see, not feel, how beautiful they are!

(*Dejection*)

Thus Baudelaire:

Rien n'égale en longueur les boiteuses journées
Quand sous les lourds flocons des neigeuses années
L'ennui, fruit de la morne incuriosité,
Prend les proportions de l'immortalité.

—Désormais tu n'es plus, o matière vivante!
Qu'un granit entouré d'une vague épouvante,
Assoupi dans le fond d'un Sahara brumeux!
Un vieux sphinx ignoré du monde insoucieux,
Oublié sur la carte, et dont l'humeur farouche
Ne chante qu'aux rayons du soleil qui se couche!

(*Spleen*)

Thus Melville:

It is a damp drizzly November in my soul;—I find myself
involuntarily pausing before coffin warehouses, and bringing
up the rear of every funeral I meet . . . it requires a strong
moral principle to prevent me from deliberately stepping into
the street, and methodically knocking people's hats off.

(*Moby Dick.* Chapter I)

And Mallarmé in a sentence:

La chair est triste, hélas! et j'ai lu tous les livres.

The grand explanatory image of this condition is of course Dürer's *Melancholia*. She sits unable to sleep and yet unable to work, surrounded by unfinished works and unused tools, the potential fragments of the city which she has the knowledge but not the will to build, tormented by a batlike creature with a board, bearing figures, and, behind her, a dark sea, a rainbow and a comet.

What is the cause of her suffering? That, surrounded by every possibility, she cannot find within herself or without the necessity to realise one rather than another. Urban society is, like the desert, a place without limits. The city walls of tradition, mythos and cultus have crumbled. There is no direction in which Ishmael is forbidden or forcibly prevented from moving. The only outside "necessities" are the random winds of fashion or the lifeless chains of a meaningless job, which, so long as he remains an individual, he can and will reject. At the same time, however, he fails to find a necessity within himself to take their place. So he must take drastic measures and go down to the waters, though in a very different sense from those of which St. John of the Cross speaks:

> *Y el cerco sosegaba*
> *Y la caballeria*
> *A vista de las aguas descendia*

37

The siege was intermitted and the cavalry dismounted at the sight of the waters.

Song of the Soul and the Bridegroom

For the waters to which Ishmael goes are bitter and medicinal.

> God help me! save I take my part
> Of danger on the roaring sea,
> A devil rises in my heart
> Far worse than any death to me.
>
> (Tennyson *The Sailor Boy*)

Fleeing to the ship where "the sons of adversity meet the children of calamity and the children of calamity meet the offspring of sin," yet at least, facing a common death, he and they are bound into a true community, so unlike the landsmen children of Abel of whom Baudelaire says

> *Race d'Abel tu croîs et broutes*
> *Comme les punaises des bois.*

And then out to sea, for there in the ocean wastes, the Paternal Power may still be felt though but as dreadful tempest, and there still dwells the Mother-Goddess though she appear but in her most malignant aspects, as the castrating white whale to Ahab, as the Life-in-Death to the Ancient Mariner

> Her lips were red, her looks were free
> Her locks were yellow as gold:
> Her skin was white as leprosy.

as the ghoul Ice-maiden to Gordon Pym.

"And now we rushed into the embrace of the cataract where a chasm threw itself open to receive us. But there arose in our pathway a shrouded human figure, very far larger in its proportions than any dweller among men. And the hue of the skin of the figure was of the perfect whiteness of snow."

Or, worst of all, the dreadful Boojum of Nothingness. Shipwreck is probable, but at least it will be a positive Death.

> *Je partirai! steamer balançant ta mâture*
> *Lève l'ancre pour une exotique nature!*
> *Un Ennui, désolé par les cruels espoirs,*
> *Croit encore à l'adieu suprême des mouchoirs!*
> *Et, peut-être, les mâts, invitant les orages,*
> *Sont-ils de ceux qu'un vent penche sur les naufrages*
> *Perdus, sans mâts, sans mâts, ni fertiles îlots . . .*
> *Mais, ô mon coeur, entends les chants des matelots.*
>
> (Mallarmé)

TWO

The Stone and the Shell

"The Non-Limited is the original material of existing things; further, the source from which existing things derive their existence is also that to which they return at their destruction, according to necessity; for they give justice and make reparation to one another for their injustice, according to the arrangement of Time."

ANAXIMANDER OF MILETUS.

"The nature of Number and Harmony admits of no Falsehood; for this is unrelated to them. Falsehood and Envy belong to the nature of the Non-Limited and the Unintelligent and the Irrational."

PHILOLAUS OF TARENTUM.

THE DESERT KNIGHT OF WORDSWORTH'S DREAM WAS
hurrying away to hide two treasures, a stone and a shell,
and the poet is quite explicit as to their significance.
The stone is geometric truth, which holds acquaintance
with the stars and weds man to man

                    "by purest bond
      Of nature undisturbed by space or time."

For it is   An image, not unworthy of the one
      Surpassing life which out of space and time
      Nor touched by weltering of passion is
      And has the name of God.

And the shell is Poetic Truth, the truth built by

                  passion which itself
      Is highest reason in a soul sublime
for it is   a god, yea many gods
has   voices more than all the winds
and is   a joy, a consolation and a hope

Further he says quite definitely that the shell is of more
worth than the stone.

As symbolic object, the stone is related to the desert,

which like the Ancient Mariner's situation is a becalmed state when the distress is caused by lack of passion, good or bad, and the shell is related to the sea, to powers, that is, which, though preferable to aridity, are nevertheless more dangerous; the shell is a consolation yet what it says is a prophecy of destruction by the weltering flood; and only a sublime soul can ride the storm.

The poet himself indeed is often endangered by his shell, and in the Seventh Book Wordsworth speaks of his interest in geometry in the following terms

> Mighty is the charm
> Of these abstractions to a mind beset
> With images and haunted by itself

and then compares himself with a shipwrecked mariner who passed the time on a desert island drawing diagrams with a stick, escaping from the distress of his corporal situation into

> an independent world
> Created out of pure intelligence.

The Whale of Truth is "for salamander giants only to encounter," and thinking can be as dangerous as feeling. He who is merely a provincial, one of those "romantic, melancholy, and absent-minded young men, disgusted with the carking cares of earth" must beware of gazing too long at the sea or the fire, for even as he takes "the mystic ocean at his feet for the visible image of that deep, blue, bottomless soul pervading mankind and nature" he is hovering over Descartian vortices

and perhaps at midday, in the fairest weather, with one half-throttled shriek you drop through that transparent air into the summer sea, no more to rise for ever,

(Moby Dick. Chapter xxxv)

the fate, for instance, of the timid child Pip, who against his own will was cast into the sea, saw "God's foot upon the treadle of the loom" and went mad, the fate of the over-sensitive Cowper:

> No voice divine the storm allay'd,
>   No light propitious shone,
> When, snatched from all effectual aid,
>   We perished, each alone:
> But I beneath a rougher sea
> And whelmed in deeper gulphs than he.
>
> (The Castaway)

When the preself-conscious savage Tashtego falls into the cistern of the sperm-whale head and is nearly drowned, Ishmael remarks, "How many, think ye, have likewise fallen into Plato's honey head, and sweetly perished there?" Even the hero may perish: the baker for all his courage vanishes away when he encounters the Boojum; and tough Baudelaire notes in his journal, "I have cultivated my hysteria with delight and terror. Now I suffer continually from vertigo, and today, the 23rd of January 1862, I have received a singular warning. I have felt the wind of the wing of madness pass over me."

THE STONE, THE SHELL AND
THE CITY

In Wordsworth's dream, then, as in all dreams, there
are a number of ambiguities.

1) The stone and the shell are alike in that they both
   signify Truth. They are also opposites. The stone is
   valuable because it stands for freedom from disorder
   and passion. The shell is valuable because it stands
   for life-giving power. Incidentally, also, the stone
   stands for the Divine Unity, the shell for the Divine
   Multiplicity.

2) Both are the means through which the True City is
   built. Men become brothers through the recognition
   of a common truth in their several minds, and
   through the experience of a common hope and joy
   in their several hearts. But at the same time both
   are dangers to the city. The truths of abstraction
   are unrelated to the historical reality of the human
   moment and distract from the historical task. The
   truths of feeling may overwhelm individual identity
   and social order in an anarchic deluge.

THE POLEMICAL SITUATION OF
ROMANTICISM

For every individual the present moment is a polemical situation, and his battle is always on two fronts: he
has to fight against his own past, not only his personal

past but also those elements in the previous generation with which he is personally involved—in the case of a poet, for instance, the poetic tradition and attitudes of the preceding generation—and simultaneously he has to fight against the present of others, who are a threat to him, against the beliefs and attitudes of the society in which he lives which are hostile to his conception of art. In order to plunge straight away into this question, let us take a few statements by that highly polemical writer William Blake.

"Cowper came to me and said: O that I were insane always. . . . Can you not make me truly insane? I will never rest till I am so. O that in the bosom of God I was hid. You claim health and yet are as mad as any of us all . . . mad as a refuge from unbelief—from Bacon, Newton and Locke."

> Mock on, Mock on Voltaire, Rousseau:
> Mock on, Mock on: 'tis all in vain!
> You throw the sand against the wind,
> And the wind blows it back again. . . .
>
> The Atoms of Democritus
> And Newton's Particles of light
> Are sands upon the Red sea shore
> Where Israel's tents do shine so bright.

"The bounded is loathed by its possessor. The same dull round, even of a universe, would soon become a mill with complicated wheels."

"Doctor Thornton's Tory Translation, Translated out of its disguise in the Classical & Scotch languages into the vulgar English.

"Our Father Augustus Caesar, who art in these thy Substantial Astronomical Telescopic Heavens, Holiness to thy Name or Title, & reverence to thy Shadow. Thy Kingship come upon Earth first & then in Heaven. Give us day by day our Real Taxed Substantial Money bought Bread; deliver from the Holy Ghost whatever cannot be Taxed; for all is debts & Taxes between Caesar & us & one anothe ; lead us not to read the Bible, but let our Bible be Virgil ⟨ Shakespeare; & deliver us from Poverty in Jesus, that Evil One. For thine is the Kingship, (or) Allegorical Godship, & the Power, or War, & the Glory, or Law, Ages after Ages in thy descendants; for God is only an Allegory of Kings & nothing Else.   Amen."

and finally   That God is Colouring Newton does shew,
                   And the devil is a Black outline, all of us know.

To Blake, then, the Enemy was the sort of conception of the universe which he associates with Newton, which he regards as having disastrous psychological, religious, political and artistic consequences.

Professor Whitehead has lucidly summarised the essential features of the Newtonian cosmology as follows:

1) The universe consists of ultimate things, whose character is private, with simple location in space.
2) On these is imposed the necessity of entering into relationships with each other. This imposition is the work of God.
3) These imposed behaviour patterns are the laws of Nature.

4) You cannot discover the natures so related by any study of the laws.

5) You cannot discover the laws by inspection of the natures.

Associated with this conception there was also that of the Great Chain of Being, i.e., creation was complete, every kind of thing which could possibly exist was already there without room for the admission of any extra novelty, and arranged in an orderly and rationally comprehensible hierarchy of being.

Such a cosmology has important theological consequences. Like the orthodox Christian God and unlike the God of Plato and Aristotle, He is the creator of the world; but unlike the Christian God, and like that of Plato and Aristotle, God and the World have no real mutual relation. While the Greek Universe loves and tries to model itself on the unconscious self-sufficient god, the Newtonian Universe is the passive neutral stuff. God imposes rational order, which it obeys, but to which it does not respond, for the natural world is no longer thought of as an organism.

At first such a concept was not altogether unwelcome to theologians. To an age exhausted by religious wars, weary of unending dogmatic disputes and exasperated by fanatic individual interpretations of Scripture, here at last the possibility of peaceful consent seemed to open up. Here was a god the existence and nature of whom could be ascertained by the use of the human reason which in all sane men comes to the same conclusion, when freed from personal passion and prejudice.

Indeed through the latter half of the seventeenth century and the first half of the eighteenth, there is an attempt in every field, religion, politics, art, etc., to do for that time what their mediaeval predecessors had done for the twelfth and thirteenth centuries, i.e., to construct a new catholic church, catholic society, and catholic art, to found a new Good City on the basis of sound reason, common sense, and good taste.

If the Enlightenment was the precursor of the French Revolution, nothing could have been further from its intentions, which were profoundly conservative and pacifist. The Encyclopaedists did not dream of a new world arising out of the ashes of an old one, but of substituting reason for unreason in the ordering of a human nature and society which was permanently the same at all times. The only necessary change was to substitute for the magic-loving priest or irrational king the rational man of esprit as the leader of the good world society. As Figaro says in Beaumarchais' play:

> *Par le sort de la naissance*
> *L'un est roi, l'autre est berger;*
> *Le hasard fit leur distance;*
> *L'esprit seul peut tout changer.*
> *De vingt rois que l'on encense*
> *Le trépas brise l'autel*
> *Et Voltaire est immortel.*

The attempt failed, but the history of the preceding two hundred years shows that, insufficient for an ultimate basis as reason, sense and taste turned out to be, they were qualities of which the time stood very much in need.

It is difficult for us to be quite fair to deist theologians like Toland, the author of *Christianity Not Mysterious*, or to hymn-writers like Addison:

> What though in solemn silence, all
> Move round the dark terrestrial ball?
> What though nor real voice nor sound
> Amid their radiant orbs be found?
> In reason's ear they all rejoice,
> And utter forth a glorious voice,
> For ever singing as they shine,
> The hand that made us is divine.

or to the rather cheap sneers of Gibbon or Voltaire, unless we remember the actual horrors of persecution, witch-hunting, and provincial superstition from which they were trying to deliver mankind. Further, the reaction of the Romantics against them is a proof that up to a point they had succeeded. If the final result of their labors was a desert, they had at least drained some very putrid marshes.

However, as Whitehead wittily remarks, such a world view is very easy to understand and extremely difficult to believe.

A transcendent God of Nature of the Newtonian type can be related to the human reason by his intelligibility, and to matter by his power to command exact obedience; the trouble begins when the question is raised of his relation to the human heart, which can and does suffer, and to the human will, which can and does disobey.

Such a Supreme Being could be completely indifferent to human joy or misery, but then he cannot possibly be identified with the Christian God who cares for men and demands their love, worship, and obedience. The attempt so to identify them must result in the purely authoritarian Judge who decrees the moral law and impartially punishes the offender, in fact, the Jehovah, God of This World, whom Blake so detested.

If the moral law is to be completely rational, there can be no contradiction between virtue and practical utility, there cannot be a kingdom of heaven whose values are completely other than the kingdom of this world. In teaching the recalcitrant to resist temptation, it becomes almost inevitable that the reason given will be that virtue succeeds and that vice fails, the Parables offered will be, in fact, the progress of the Virtuous Apprentice who finally marries the master's daughter and the progress of the Rake who ends in Bedlam. Children will be made to pay special attention to such verses as:

> Like some fair tree which, fed by streams
>   With timely fruit doth bend;
> He still shall flourish, and success
>   All his designs attend.
>
> Ungodly men in their attempts
>   No lasting roots shall find

Untimely, withered and dispersed
Like chaff before the wind.

(Tate and Brady, Psalm 1.)

With his usual unerring insight Blake saw that the crucial points at issue were the Incarnation of Christ and the Forgiveness of Sins. A Supreme Architect cannot incarnate as an individual, only as the whole building; and a pure Judge cannot forgive; he can only condemn or acquit.

Blake and the other romantics along with him tried in their reaction, not to overcome the dualism, but to stand it on its head,* i.e., to make God purely immanent, so that to Blake God only acts and is in existing beings and men, or is pantheistically diffused through physical nature, not to be perceived by any exercise of the reason, but only through vision and feeling.

---

* More accurately, they absolutise another mode of consciousness. The deist God is an absolutisation of the ego's consciousness of itself as stretching beyond itself, of standing as a spectator apprehending an external reality. The romantic immanent God, on the other hand, is an absolutisation of the ego's consciousness of itself as self-contained, as embracing all of which it is aware in a unity of experiencing. In Hegel, the third mode of consciousness, the ego's consciousness of itself as striving towards is similarly exalted at the expense of the other two modes.

One might say that in deist theology the Son is called the Father and the divinity of the Father is denied, while in romantic theology the divinity of the Son is denied and the Father might more properly be called the Mother.

For a discussion of these heresies in the light of the Catholic teaching of the analogical relation between the Deity and creation see *Polarity* by Erich Przywara (Oxford, 1935), and for the relevance of the Athanasian creed to the artist *The Mind of the Maker* by Dorothy Sayers (Harcourt Brace, 1941).

So Coleridge writes:

> In the Hebrew poets each thing has a life of its own and
> yet they are all one life. In God they move and live and *have*
> their being; not *had*, as the cold system of Newtonian Theo-
> logy represents, but *have*.

As to the Great Chain of Being, it is retained but in a
quite different spirit. The fullness of the universe is felt
to be irrational but that is its charm. Thus Schiller
writes:

> Every kind of perfection must attain existence in the full-
> ness of the world . . . in the infinite chasm of nature no
> activity could be omitted, no grade of enjoyment be wanting
> in the universal happiness . . . the Great Inventor could not
> permit even error to remain unutilized in his great design . . .
> It is a provision of the supreme wisdom that erring reason
> should people even the chaotic land of dreams and should
> cultivate even the barren land of contradiction . . . *Life* and
> *Liberty* to the greatest possible extent are the glory of the
> divine creation; nowhere is it more sublime than where it
> seems to have departed most widely from its ideal.

So too with the problem of evil and suffering. The
attempt to explain either in rational terms alone, i.e., as
if the question "Why do they exist?" were one primarily
raised by the intellect, the substitution for Providence
and Wisdom of Economy and Utility, created mysteries
more fantastic than any which it replaced, e.g., the
suggestion of Soame Jenyns that there might be higher
beings who torment us for their pleasure and utility

in the same way that we hunt animals, in reply to which Dr. Johnson composed a famous passage:

"As we drown whelps and kittens, they amuse themselves now and then with sinking a ship, and stand round the fields of Blenheim or the walls of Prague, as we encircle a cock-pit. As we shoot a bird flying, they take a man in the midst of his business or pleasure, and knock him down with an apoplexy. Some of them, perhaps, are virtuosi, and delight in the operations of an asthma, as a human philosopher in the effects of the air-pump. To swell a man with a tympany is as good sport as to blow a frog. Many a merry bout have these frolick beings at the vicissitudes of an ague, and good sport it is to see a man tumble with an epilepsy, and revive and tumble again, and all this he knows not why. As they are wiser and more powerful than we, they have more exquisite diversions, for we have no way of procuring any sport so brisk and so lasting, as the paroxysms of the gout and stone, which undoubtedly must make high mirth, especially if the play be a little diversified with the blunders and puzzles of the blind and deaf."

If such were true, then the only decent human reaction can be that of Captain Ahab, defiance till death.

The Romantic reaction to this is twofold. When they are objecting to the moralist legalism which thought in terms of objective infractions of the moral law and its appropriate penalties, they produce the figure of the Prelapsarian savage (Queequeg), the innocent sailor (Budd), or the child of the Immortality Ode, whose heart is good though he does not consciously understand or even keep the moral law of the Pharisee. When, on the other hand, they are objecting to the rationalistic optimism which attributes evil to mental ignorance curable by education, they reassert the fallen nature of men and the necessity for conversion.

To the Deists, who thought, like John Sheffield, Duke of Buckingham:

> While in dark Ignorance we lay afraid
> Of Fancies, Ghosts in every empty shade,
> Great Hobbes appeared and by plain Reason's light
> Put such phantastick Forms to shameful Flight.
> Fond is their Fear who think Man needs must be
> To Vice enslaved, if from vain Terrors free:
> The Wise and Good, Morality shall guide
> And Superstition all the World beside.

Blake retorts:

"Man is born a Spectre or Satan and is altogether an Evil, and requires a New Selfhood continually, and must continually be changed into his direct contrary. But your Greek Philosophy (which is a remnant of Druidism) teaches that Man is Righteous in his Vegetated Spectre. . . . Voltaire Rousseau. . . . you are Pharisees and Hypocrites, for you are constantly talking of the Virtues of the Human Heart and particularly of your own, that you may accuse others."

(Jerusalem)

And Baudelaire to the disciples of Voltaire:

"Belief in Progress is a doctrine of idlers and Belgians. . . . True civilisation is not to be found in gas or steam or table-turning. It consists in the diminution of the traces of original sin."

(Mon Coeur Mis à Nu)

POLITICS AND INDIVIDUALISM

Just as it had sought to escape from sectarian fanaticism by establishing a catholic religion of the One Engineer, so the eighteenth century sought to escape from the arbitrariness of absolute monarchy by establishing a catholic society in which all men were equal because they all possessed a body and a mind which obeyed and recognised the same laws. But this over-simplified the nature of man; by denying him an individual soul or by identifying soul with mind, it did indeed make men equal, but with the equality of billiard-balls, not of individual persons. To such a doctrine of a natural law which self-interest guided by common sense will of course accept, the proper answer is that of the hero of Dostoevsky's *Notes from Underground:*

"You will scream at me (that is if you condescend to do so) that no one is touching my free will, that all they are concerned with is that my will should of itself, of its own free will, coincide with my own normal interests, with the laws of nature and arithmetic. Good heavens, gentlemen, what sort of free will is left when we come to tabulation and arithmetic, when it will all be a case of twice two makes four? Twice two makes four without my will. As if free will meant that."

Hence the Romantic reaction stressed the soul and its uniqueness; Herder propounds the uniqueness of the soul of a nation; Schlegel writes: "It is precisely individuality that is the original and eternal theory in men." Novalis declares: "The more personal, local, peculiar, of its own time a poem is, the nearer it stands to the centre of poetry."

Minds may be similar, but they are not the whole or even the chief element in a human being. "I would rather," says Ishmael, "feel your spine than your skull, whoever you are."

The Deist religion of reason had a catholic myth, that of the Goddess of reason, but no cultus, no specifically religious acts; all rational acts were worship of the Goddess.

The romantic reaction replaced the Goddess by a protestant variety of individual myths; but it, too, lacked a cult in which all men could take part. Instead, it substituted imagination for reason, and in place of the man of esprit the artist as the priest-magician.

> Art is the tree of life. Art is Christianity.
>> says Blake.

> Poets are the unacknowledged legislators of the world.
>> says Shelley.

And when Baudelaire says:

> There are no great men save the poet, the priest, and the soldier . . . the rest are born for the whip.
>> (*Mon Coeur Mis à Nu*)

one is not convinced that he cares as much about the last two as about the first.

ROMANTIC AESTHETIC THEORY

Cartesian metaphysics, Newtonian physics and eighteenth-century theories of perception divided the body from the mind, and the primary objects of perception from their secondary qualities, so that physical nature became, as Professor Collingwood says, "matter, infinite in extent, permeated by movement, devoid of ultimate qualitative differences, and moved by uniform and purely quantitative forces," the colorless desert from which Melville recoils:

"All deified nature absolutely paints like a harlot, whose allurements cover nothing but the charnel house within; and when we proceed further, the palsied universe lies before us like a leper."

(Moby Dick. Chapter LXII)

Such a view must naturally affect the theory of artistic composition, for it involves a similar division between the thing to be expressed and the medium in which it is expressed.

"Memory," writes Hobbes, "is the World in which the Judgement, the severer sister, busieth herself in a grave and rigid examination of all the parts of nature and in registering by letters their order, causes, uses, differences, and resemblances; whereby the Fancy, when any work of Art is to be performed, finding her materials at hand and prepared for use, needs no more than a swift motion over them, that what she wants and is there to be had, may not lie too long unespied."

And Dryden:

"Expression and all that belongs to words is that in a poem which coloring is in a picture . . . Expression is, in plain English, the bawd of her sister, the design . . . she clothes, she dresses her up, she paints her, she makes her appear more lovely than she is."

(Poetry and Painting)

This makes artistic creation an entirely conscious process, and here again we shall not understand its appeal to such great poets as Dryden and Pope unless we understand their wish to escape from chaotic idiosyncrasies, their hope of establishing catholic and objective canons of good taste recognisable by poets and public alike. Given the subjects with which these poets were passionately concerned—e.g., Dryden was as moved by the play of dialectic as Wordsworth was by Nature, Pope saw in Dulness as great a threat to the City as Dante saw in Sin—the theory did no harm; indeed it did good, for there is a conscious side of creation, and it made the poets take pains at a time when such pains were needed.

A Poem where we all perfections find
Is not the work of a Fantastick mind:

> There must be Care, and Time, and Skill, and Pains;
> Not the first heat of unexperienced brains
> > (Roscommon)

is sound advice.

It was only when poets continued working on the same themes as Dryden and Pope but without their passion, or attempted other kinds of themes to which this diction and treatment were unsuited that the deficiencies of the theory became apparent.

The Romantic reaction, naturally, was to stress imagination and vision; i.e., the less conscious side of artistic creation, the uniqueness of the poet's individual experience, and the symbolic rather than the decorative or descriptive value of images. "What is the modern conception of Art?" asks Baudelaire. "To create a suggestive magic including at the same time object and subject, the world outside the artist and the artist himself." "What is a poet if not a translator, a decipherer?"

THE ROMANTIC USE OF SYMBOLS

To understand the romantic conception of the relation between objective and subjective experience, *Moby Dick* is perhaps the best work to study, partly because in certain aspects it includes preromantic attitudes and treatments which show off the former more clearly than a purely romantic work like *The Ancient Mariner* or *Gordon Pym*.

If we omit the White Whale itself, the whole book is

an elaborate synecdoche, i.e., it takes a particular way of life, that of whale-fishing, which men actually lead to earn their livelihood and of which Melville had first-hand experience and makes it a case of any man's life in general. This literary device is an old one and can be found at all periods; indeed almost all literature does this.

E.g.

1) Whalemen kill for their living. So in one way or another must we all.

2) The proprietors of the *Pequod* are Quakers, i.e., they profess the purest doctrine of non-violence, yet see no incongruity in this; though perhaps Peleg recognises the paradox indirectly when he says: "Pious Harpooners never make good voyages. It takes the shark out of them." So always in every life, except that of the saint or the villain, there is a vast difference between what a man professes and how he acts.

3) The crew are involved in each other's actions and characters. So every world is a world of social relations.

4) In their attitude towards their job of killing whales, they reveal their different characters. Thus Starbuck is a professional who takes no risks unless he has to and will have no man in his boat who is not afraid of the whale. Stubb is a reckless gambler who enjoys risks. Flask follows the fish just for the fun of it.

Insofar as the book is this, any other form of activity or

society which Melville happened to know well would have served his purpose.

Then *Moby Dick* is full of parable and typology, i.e., as X is in one field of experience, so is Y in another. E.g.

"All men live enveloped in whale-lines. All are born with halters round their necks; but it is only when caught in the soft, sudden turn of death that mortals realise the silent subtle ever-present perils of life."

(Chapter LX)

or

"O men, admire—model thyself after the whale. Do thou too remain warm among ice. Do thou, too, live in this world without being of it. Be cool at the Equator, keep thy blood flow at the Pole and retain in all seasons a temperature of thine own."

(Chapter LXVIII)

or again the characters and names of the nine ships (the number is symbol not allegory) which the *Pequod* encounters are, in their relation to Moby Dick, types of the relation of human individuals and societies in the tragic mystery of existence. I.e.,

The *Goney*   The aged who may have experienced the mystery but cannot tell others. (The captain's trumpet falls into the sea.)

63

The *Town-Ho*	Those who have knowledge of the mystery but keep it secret. (No one tells Ahab the story of Radney and Steelkilt.)
The *Jeroboam*	Those who make a superstitious idolatry of the mystery or whom the mystery has driven crazy.
The *Jungfrau* and the *Rosebud*	Those who out of sloth and avarice respectively will never become aware of the mystery.
The *Enderby*	Those who are aware of the mystery but face it with rational common sense and stoicism. ("What you take for the White Whale's malice is only his awkwardness.")
The *Bachelor*	The frivolous and fortunate who deny the existence of the mystery. ("Have heard of Moby Dick but don't believe in him at all.")
The *Rachel*	Those who have without their understanding or choice become involved in the mystery as the innocents massacred by Herod were involved in the birth of Christ.
The *Delight*	Those whose encounter with the mystery has turned their joy into sorrow.

This analogical method was practised by the Church Fathers in their interpretations of Scripture, and analogies from nature have been common ever since, for exam-

ple in the Mediaeval Bestiaries or Jonathan Edwards'
Images or Shadows of Divine Things. It is a conscious
process, calling for Judgment and Fancy rather than
Imagination, and the one-to-one correspondence as-
serted is grasped by the reader's reason.

Lastly, in his treatment of the White Whale, Melville
uses symbols in the real sense.

A symbol is felt to be such before any possible meaning is consciously recognised; i.e., an object or event
which is felt to be more important than the reason can
immediately explain is symbolic. Secondly, a symbolic
correspondence is never one to one but always multiple,
and different persons perceive different meanings. Thus
to Ahab "All visible objects, man, are but pasteboard
masks. To me the white whale is that wall shoved near
to me. Sometimes I think there's naught beyond. I see
in him outrageous strength with an insatiable malice
sinewing it. That inscrutable thing is chiefly what I
hate."

To Gabriel, the mad demagogue who terrorises the
Jeroboam, its qualities are similar, but his attitude is
one of positive idolisation. He worships it as an incarnation of the Shaker God. To Steelkilt of the *Town-Ho*
it is the justice and mercy of God, saving him from
becoming a murderer and slaying the unjust Radney.
To Melville-Ishmael it is neither evil nor good but
simply numinous, a declaration of the power and
majesty of God which transcends any human standards
of ethics. To Starbuck it signifies death or his fatal

relation to his captain, the duty which tells him he cannot depart his office to obey, intending open war, yet to have a touch of pity.

THE SHIP AS SYMBOL

If thought of as isolated in the midst of the ocean, a ship can stand for mankind and human society moving through time and struggling with its destiny. If thought of as leaving the land for the ocean, it stands for a particular kind of man and society as contrasted with the average landdwelling kind. *The Hunting of the Snark* is a pure example of the first use, *Twenty Thousand Leagues under the Sea* of the second. In Melville's books, and this is one of the reasons for their fascination, there is a constant interplay between both.

THE SHIP AS MANKIND

A constant aesthetic problem for the writer is how to reconcile his desire to include everything, not to leave anything important out, with his desire for an aesthetic whole, that there shall be no irrelevances and loose ends. The picture has to be both complete and framed. The more society becomes differentiated through division of labor, the more it becomes atomised through urbanisation and through greater ease of communication, the harder it becomes for the artist to find a satisfactory solution.

For, of the traditional wholes, the family becomes representative of one class only, the village the exceptional way of life instead of the typical. The ship is one of the few possible devices left, because, while it is most emphatically a frame—no one can get off or on board once the ship has started—yet it permits of a great deal of variety and interpretation.

E.g.

1) The people on board can show every variety of character as individuals and every age of man from fourteen to seventy. "Wrecked on a desert shore, a man of war's crew could quickly form an Alexandria for themselves."

2) There are a number of social grades: Captain—Mates—Harpooners—Seamen, so that the role of authority in human society and of its dialectical relation to character can be portrayed.

3) A ship has a function to perform, to hunt whales, to fight battles etc., and each member of the crew has his specialised function. The carpenter must carpenter, the boatswain must flog, the chaplain must preach, the master at arms must spy, etc., which allow the exhibition of all the relations between functions, given or chosen, and the character which willingly or unwillingly performs it.

There can even be passengers without a function.

4) Life on a ship exhibits the distinction and relation between society, i.e., human beings associated for an end, and community, human beings associated

by the tie of a common love or interest. Thus on
The Neversink there are a number of antagonistic
communities within the common society, for instance, the officers versus the common seamen, the
rulers whose orders cannot be questioned and the
ruled who feel like Melville:

"I was a Roman Jew of the Middle Ages confined to the
Jewish quarter of the town and forbidden to stray beyond
its limits."

"by far the majority of the common sailors of the *Neversink*
were plainly concerned at the prospect of war and were plainly
averse to it. But with the officers of the quarterdeck it was
just the reverse . . . Because, though war would equally
jeopardise the lives of both, yet, while it held out to the
sailor no promise of promotion, and what is called *glory*, these
things fired the heart of his officers."

(*White Jacket*)

In the case of the *Pequod*, the situation at the beginning is this: All of the crew with the exception of the
captain are a community in that they all want to
hunt whales and make money; Ahab stands outside,
having no wish to hunt any whale except Moby
Dick. He is so far from wishing to make a profitable
voyage that, when the barrels begin leaking he would
prefer to let them leak rather than delay his quest
and only yields to Starbuck's demand to "up Bur-
tons" because he is afraid of mutiny. At the end,
however, Ahab has so infected the crew with his pas-

sion that they have ceased to care what happens
and are made one community with him.

"They were one man, not thirty. For as the one ship that
held them all; though it was put together of all contrasting
things—oak, and maple, and pine wood; iron, and pitch, and
hemp—yet all these ran into each other in the one concrete
hull, which shot on its way, both balanced and directed by
the long central keel; even so, all the individualities of the
crew, this man's valor, that man's fear; guilt and guiltiness,
all varieties were welded into oneness, and were all directed
to that fatal goal which Ahab their one lord and keel did
point to."

(*Moby Dick*. Chapter cxxxiv)

5) As a society which, once you are in (the question of
how you get in is only raised when the ship is used
in the second symbolic sense of a special kind of life)
you cannot get out of, whether you like it or not,
whether you approve of it or not, a ship can represent either:

a) The state of being human as decreed by God.
Mutiny then is a symbol of the original rebellion
of Lucifer and of Adam, the refusal to accept fin-
itude and dependence.

b) The *civitas terrena*, created by self-love, in-
herited and repeated, into which all men since
Adam are born, yet where they have never
totally lost their knowledge of and longing for
the Civitas Dei and the Law of Love. From this
arise absurd contradictions, like the chaplain on

a man-of-war who is paid a share of the reward
for sinking a ship and cannot condemn war or
flogging, or the devout Baptist who earns his
bread as captain of a gun.

To be like Christ, to obey the law of love absolutely, is possible only for the saint, for Billy
Budd, and even for him the consequence is the
same as for Christ, crucifixion. The rest of us cannot avoid disingenuous compliances. Thus, in his
dissertation on Chronometricals and Horologi-
cals in *Pierre*, Melville writes:

"Bacon's brains were mere watch-maker's brains; but
Christ was a chronometer . . . And the reason why His
teachings seemed folly to the Jews, was because he carried
that Heaven's time in Jerusalem, while the Jews carried
Jerusalem time there . . . as the China watches are right as
to China, so the Greenwich chronometers must be wrong as
to China. Besides, of what use to the Chinaman would a
Greenwich chronometer, keeping Greenwich time, be? Were
he thereby to regulate his daily actions, he would be guilty of
all manner of absurdities:—going to bed at noon, say, when
his neighbors would be sitting down to dinner.*

". . . one thing is to be especially observed. Though Christ
encountered woe in both the precept and the practice of His
chronometricals, yet did He remain throughout entirely without folly or sin. Whereas, almost invariably, with inferior be-

---

* Cf. the snark

  Its habit of getting up late you'll agree
  That it carries too far when I say
  That it frequently breakfasts at five-o-clock tea
  And dines on the following day.

ings, the absolute effort to live in this world according to the strict letter of the chronometricals is, somehow, apt to involve those inferior beings eventually in strange, *unique* follies and sins, unimagined before."

THE SHIP VERSUS THE CITY

In so far as a ship and its crew sail, whether gladly or sadly, away from the land, where all were born, and leave the majority, whether friends or foes, behind on shore, the mariner image has a different constellation of meanings.

1) *The Search for Possibility and the Escape from Necessity*

Land is the place where people are born, marry, and have children, the world where the changing seasons create a round of different duties and feelings, and the ocean, by contrast, is the place where there are no ties of home or sex, only of duty to the end for which the voyage is undertaken, the world where the change of seasons makes no difference to what the crew must do and where there is no visible life other than theirs, so that to leave land and put out to sea can signify the freeing of the spirit from finite nature, its ascetic denial of the flesh, the determination to live in one-directional historical time rather than in cyclical natural time.

e.g.   *Verse-nous ton poison pour qu'il nous réconforte!*
Nous voulons, tant ce feu nous brûle le cerveau

71

> *Plonger au fond du gouffre, Enfer ou Ciel, qu'importe*
> *Au fond de l'Inconnu pour trouver du nouveau.*
>
> (*Le Voyage*)

i.e. the flight from finite repetition to infinite novelty.

> *Plus douce qu'aux enfants la chair des pommes sures,*
> *L'eau verte pénétra ma coque de sapin*
> *Et des taches de vins bleus et des vomissures*
> *Me lava, dispersant gouvernail et grappin.*
>
> (*Bâteau Ivre*)

> *Pour n'être pas changés en bêtes, ils s'enivrent*
> *D'espace et de lumière et de cieux embrasés;*
> *La glace qui les mord, les soleils qui les cuivrent,*
> *Effacent lentement la marque des baisers.*
>
> (*Le Voyage*)

i.e., the purification from debauchery and sex. "The *Nautilus* is a place of refuge for those who, like its commander, have broken every tie upon earth."

i.e., the flight from injustice.

". . . Come hither, broken-hearted; here is another life without the guilt of intermediate death; here are wonders supernatural, without dying for them. Come hither! bury thyself in a life which, to your now equally abhorred and abhorring, landed world, is more oblivious than death. Come hither! put up thy grave-stone, too, within the churchyard, and come hither, till we marry thee!"

Hearkening to these voices, East and West, by early sun-

rise, and by fall of eve, the blacksmith's soul responded, Aye,
I come! And so Perth went a-whaling.

(Moby Dick. Chap. CXII)

i.e., the flight from memory.

Away O soul! hoist instantly the anchor!
Cut the hawsers—haul out—shake out every sail!
Have we not stood here like trees in the ground long enough?
Have we not grovel'd here long enough, eating and drinking
  like mere brutes?
Have we not darken'd and dazed ourselves with books long
  enough?

Sail forth—steer for the deep waters only,
Reckless O soul, exploring, I with thee, and thou with me.
For we are bound where mariner has not yet dared to go.
And we will risk the ship, ourselves and all.

(Passage to India)

i.e., the rejection of conventional habit.

2) *The Search for Necessity and the Escape from Possibility*

The fact that a ship is a strictly disciplined and authoritarian society as compared with normal life, and that a ship has a purpose for a voyage, means that ship and city can have almost exactly the opposite significance to the above, i.e., the land can be thought of as the

noir océan de l'immonde cité,

the place of purposelessness, of the ennui that comes

73

from being confronted with infinite possibilities
without the necessity to choose one.

So, for instance, in Ishmael's case, or in Melville's
enlistment on the *Neversink*, their going to sea is a
commitment to a necessity which, however unpleasant, is at least certain and preferable to the
melancholia and accidie induced by the meaningless
freedom on shore.

THE ENVIRONMENT OF THE SHIP

The ship, i.e., the human, individual or social, is
related to two pairs of contrasting symbols, i.e.,

A. The sky and its crea- vs. The water and its
tures, birds   creatures, fish, whales,
                                 octopuses, etc.

B. The day and the sun vs. The night and the
and to two scales of   moon
weather.
The degree of visibility.   From very clear to
                                thick fog.

The velocity of the   From typhoon to dead
wind.   calm.

The symbolism is easier to grasp in the purely imaginary
voyages like those of Coleridge, Baudelaire and Rimbaud than in the work of Melville and Hopkins, where

there is the extra complication of the relation of objective reality to subjective meaning.

A

Sky as contrasted with water = Spirit as contrasted with Nature.

What comes from the sky is a spiritual or supernatural visitation.

What lies hidden in the water is the unknown powers of nature.

E.g.

Cp. the angelic spirits sent by the Moon, or Master of the sea, who move the Ancient Mariner's ship by removing the air in front of it, and the avenging spirit from the land of ice and snow which dwells nine fathoms below the surface and at their command unwillingly moves the ship up to the line.

Cp. The Albatross which is related to the Dove of the Holy Spirit, and through him to the innocent victim, Christ, the water-snakes which are that in nature, whether outside man or within himself, for which he feels aversion because he cannot understand them aesthetically or intellectually and despises because he cannot make use of them. But for the Fall (the shooting of the Albatross), Adam (The Ancient Mariner) would never have consciously learned through suffering the meaning of Agapé, i.e., to love one's neighbour as oneself without comparisons or greed (the blessing of the snakes), so that the Ancient Mariner might well say in the end, *O felix culpa.*

Similarly the hawk in *Moby Dick* is the messenger bird of Zeus who warns Prometheus-Ahab of his hybris when he cheats the lookout by snatching away his hat, i.e., his heroic crown, but whom in its last death-defiance the *Pequod* drags down with it. Contrasted with him is the great squid, messenger of the underworld, whose appearance frightens Starbuck more than the whale itself.

In *Un Voyage à Cythère*, the doves of Venus have been metamorphosed into ferocious crows who devour the male corpse.

B

Day and the Sun = Consciousness and the Paternal Principle as contrasted with

Night and the Moon = Unconsciousness and the Maternal Principle.

In his excellent essay on *The Ancient Mariner*,* Mr. Robert Penn Warren has pointed out how all the events of salvation take place under the influence of the moon, and that the sun is the hostile judge of conscience.

The Father Sun can appear at night in the form of lightning.

E.g.

> The thick black cloud was cleft, and still
> The Moon was at its side:

---

* The Rime of The Ancient Mariner. (Reynal & Hitchcock, 1946)

> Like waters shot from some high crag,
> The lightning fell with never a jag,
> A river steep and wide.

Here the Ancient Mariner, so afraid of the Father, is comforted by knowing that the Mother is still present. Again when Captain Ahab addresses the lightning, on a night without a moon, he says:

"Thou art my fiery father; my sweet mother I know not. What hast thou done with her?"

And Hopkins, addressing God:

> I did say yes
> O at lightning and lashed rod;
> Thou heardst me truer than tongue confess
> Thy terror, O Christ, O God;
> Thou knowest the walls, altar and hour and night:
> The swoon of a heart that the sweep and the hurl of thee
> trod
> Hard down with a horror of height:
> And the midriff astrain with leaning of, laced with fire of stress.

VISIBILITY

The degree of visibility = the degree of conscious knowledge.
I.e., fog and mist mean doubt and self-delusion, a clear day knowing where one is going or exactly what one has done.

THE WIND

The wind is always a force which the conscious will cannot cause or control. In the works we are considering which were written before the advent of the steamship, it is also the source, good or bad, of all the movements of life.

In *The Ancient Mariner* there are four winds described.

1) The tyrannous strong wind which chases the ship down to the dangerous land of icebergs, mist and snow, against her will.

> With sloping masts and dipping prow,
> As who pursued with yell and blow
> Still treads the shadow of his foe,
> And forward bends his head,
> The ship drove fast, loud roared the blast,
> And southward aye we fled.

Man, that is, is driven on by an irresistible rush of creative powers which he did not expect and which frighten him because he does not know where they are carrying him except that it is probably into a state of dread. The powers, however, are not necessarily evil. They only, as it turns out, drive him into temptation, for the icebergs represent that state of dread which Kierkegaard describes as the necessary precondition for the Fall.

Dread is a desire for what one fears, a sympathetic antipathy; dread is an alien power which takes hold of the individual, and yet one cannot extricate oneself from it, does not wish to, because one is afraid, but what one fears attracts one. Dread renders the individual powerless, and the first sin always happens in a moment of weakness; it therefore lacks any accountableness, but that want is the real snare.*

(The Concept of Dread)

2) The good south wind which extricates them from the ice. This is not frightening because it takes the ego where the ego thinks it wants to go. In fact, it turns out to be, like the first elation of Adam and Eve after eating the apple, a delusion, for it disappears and leaves them in the absolute calm of guilt and despair, bereft of all power.

3) The roaring wind which is only heard and never touches the Mariner or the ship, but brings rain, and at the sound of which angelic spirits occupy the bodies of the dead crew. To hear and not feel, means to intuit the possibility and hope for the coming of the new life which one still does not know as an actuality.

4) Finally, when his repentance is complete, so that he can even look away from the dead men (the proof of his sin), then comes the gentle wind which fans his cheek and leads the ship back home, i.e., the powers of grace and blessing.

In *Bateau Ivre*, the wind is usually violent and inevi-

---

* *The Voyage of Maeldune* begins with a similar violent wind which does just the opposite; it takes the hero intent on vengeance away from opportunity to become guilty.

table, but the point is that the hero of the poem deliberately surrenders to it. He enjoys defiantly its irrationality and disorder, and speaks of

> *tohus-bohus . . . triomphants*
> *La tempête a béni mes éveils maritimes.*
>
> *J'ai suivi, des mois pleins, pareille aux vacheries*
> *Hystériques, la houle à l'assaut des récifs,*
> *Sans songer que les pieds lumineux des Maries*
> *Pussent forcer le mufle aux Océans poussifs.*
>
> *Des écumes de fleurs ont béni mes dérades*
> *Et d'ineffables vents m'ont ailé par instants.*

The final result, however, is exhaustion, the state of all-too-real calm, and lack of relation.

> *Mais, vrai, j'ai trop pleuré. Les aubes sont navrantes,*
> *Toute lune est atroce et tout soleil amer . . .*
>
> *Je ne puis plus, baigné de vos langueurs, ô lames,*
> *Enlever leur sillage aux porteurs de cotons.*
>
> *(Bateau Ivre)*

In *Moby Dick*, where the weather is real weather in nature, the point is the relation of human nature to non-human nature, i.e., the kind of importance that the human characters attribute to it. E.g., the typhoon is significant to two of the characters, Starbuck and Ahab.

"Here!" cried Starbuck, seizing Stubb by the shoulder, and pointing his hand towards the weather bow, "markest thou not that the gale comes from the eastward, the very course

Ahab is to run for Moby Dick? . . . The gale that now hammers at us to stave us, we can turn it into a fair wind that will drive us towards home."

(Chapter CXIX)

His disapproval of Ahab's quest is strengthened by this omen to the point where he goes down to Ahab's cabin with the intention of killing him as a madman. Ahab, on the other hand, is tempted precisely because the Typhoon is in opposition to the way he has sworn to go.

"I own thy speechless, placeless power; but to the last gasp of my earthquake life will dispute its unconditional unintegral mastery in me . . . Come in thy lowest form of love, and I will kneel and kiss thee; but at thy highest, come as mere supernal power; and though thou launchest navies of full-freighted worlds, there's that in here that still remains indifferent."

(Chapter CXIX)

A calm, such as the beautiful day, before the final chase begins, which offers no outside opposition, makes him think of wife and child, and nearly wins him over to Starbuck's side and to giving up the quest.

The use of the tempest in *The Wreck of the Deutschland* is still more complicated.

We have the physical contrasted situation of Hopkins, the Jesuit novice

> Away in the loveable west,
> On a pastoral forehead of Wales,
> I was under a roof here, I was at rest,

and of the nuns

> And they the prey of the gales

and in counterpoint to this is the subjective contrast of
their inner peace in the face of death:

> Ah! there was a heart right!
> There was single eye!
> Read the unshapeable shock night
> And knew the who and the why;
> Wording it how but by him that present and past,
> Heaven and earth are word of, worded by?
> The Simon Peter of a soul! to the blast
> Tarpeian-fast, but a blown beacon of light

with his inner tempest in his struggle to submit his
self-will to the will of God, on the necessity of which
St. Ignatius lays so much importance.

> The frown of his face
> Before me, the hurtle of hell
> Behind, where, where was a, where was a place?

Both kinds of tempest are related as forms of suffering, but also carefully differentiated. The suffering
that arises out of the relation of the soul to God only
arises because of the human sin of which the climax was
the Crucifixion:

> The dense and the driven Passion, and frightful sweat;
> Thence the discharge of it, there its swelling to be,
> Though felt before, though in high flood yet—

What none would have known of it, only the heart, being hard
    at bay

The relation was intended to be one of joy, and the intensity of the struggle is a direct indication of the amount
of self-will to be overcome, i.e., spiritual suffering is to
be treated as purgatorial, i.e., the sufferer must embrace it, saying, "I say pain but ought to say solace."

External suffering, on the other hand, is something
different. No one who is shipwrecked or diseased is to be
considered as more or less sinful than fortunate people.
Nevertheless, nature is the handiwork of God.

They fought with God's cold.

All that the individual can do is accept it as he or she
must accept every other event pleasant or unpleasant
that happens to him, as a challenge, not to despair like
Starbuck, not to defy like Ahab, but as an occasion to
ask what in this actual situation sent by God God requires.

In this case the nuns who are innocent exiles

> Loathed for a love men knew in them,
> Banned by the land of their birth,
> Rhine refused them. Thames would ruin them.

by their conduct in this disaster are a witness to their
faith which in the very moment of physical destruction
may have saved some souls from spiritual death.

> Well, she has thee for the pain, for the
> Patience; but pity of the rest of them!

83

> Heart, go and bleed at a bitterer vain for the
>   Comfortless unconfessed of them—
> No not uncomforted: lovely-felicitous Providence
> Finger of a tender of, O of a feathery delicacy, the breast
>   of the
>   Maiden could obey so, be a bell to, ring of it, and
> Startle the poor sheep back! is the shipwrack then a harvest,
>   does tempest carry the grain for thee?

THE STONE, THE ROMANTICS AND MATHEMATICS

Whereas the Neoclassical writers had been taught to observe particular natural objects carefully and accurately and then abstract the general from them, the Romantics reverse the process. Thus Blake says: "All goodness resides in minute particulars" but "Natural objects always did and now do weaken, deaden and obliterate imagination in me" and Coleridge writes in a letter:

"The further I ascend from animated Nature (i.e., in the embracements of rocks and hills), from men and cattle, and the common birds of the woods and fields, the greater becomes in me the intensity of the feeling of life. Life seems to me then a universal spirit that neither has nor can have an opposite."

As long as images derived from observation of nature had a utility value for decorating the thoughts of the mind, nature could be simply enjoyed, for Nature was

not very important by comparison with human reason.
But if there is a mysterious relation between them, if

> *La Nature est un temple où de vivants piliers*
> *Laissent parfois sortir de confuses paroles;*
> *L'homme y passe à travers des forêts de symboles*
> *Qui l'observent avec des regards familiers.*
>
> *Comme de longs échos qui de loin se confondent*
> *Dans une ténébreuse et profonde unité,*
> *Vaste comme la nuit et comme la clarté,*
> *Les parfums, les couleurs et les sons se répondent,*
>
> > Baudelaire (*Correspondances*)

then the merely visual perception is not the important
act, but the intuitive vision of the meaning of the object,
and also Nature becomes a much more formidable
creature, charged with all the joys, griefs, hopes and
terrors of the human soul, and therefore arousing very
mixed feelings of love and hatred.

On the one hand, the poets long to immerse in the sea
of Nature, to enjoy its endless mystery and novelty, on
the other, they long to come to port in some transcendent eternal and unchanging reality from which the un-
expected is excluded. Nature and Passion are powerful,
but they are also full of grief. True happiness would
have the calm and order of bourgeois routine without
its utilitarian ignobility and boredom.

Thus the same Baudelaire who writes:

"Why is the spectacle of the sea so infinitely and eternally
agreeable?

"Because the sea presents at once the idea of immensity

and of movement . . . Twelve or fourteen leagues of liquid in movement are enough to convey to man the highest expression of beauty which he can encounter in his transient abode."

(Mon Coeur Mis à Nu)

and identifies human nature with the sea:

> *Vous êtes tous les deux ténébreux et discrets*
> *Homme, nul n'a sondé le fond de tes abîmes,*
> *O mer, nul ne connaît tes richesses intimes*
> *Tant vous êtes jaloux de garder vos secrets!*

(L'Homme et la Mer)

also exclaims:

> *Ah! ne jamais sortir des Nombres et des Êtres*

and likens Beauty to a dream of stone (cp. the stone of Wordsworth's dream):

> *Je hais le mouvement qui déplace les lignes,*
> *Et jamais je ne pleure et jamais je ne ris.*

And the amorous Henry Beyle who cannot live without a grand passion writes:

"I used to imagine that the higher mathematics dealt with all, or almost all, aspects of things, and that, by proceeding to their study, I should arrive at a knowledge of all things that were certain, irrefutable, and demonstrable at will. I said to myself, 'mathematics will get me out of Grenoble, out of that sickening morass.' "

So too in *The Hunting of the Snark* the Beaver and the Butcher, romantic explorers though they are, who have chosen to enter a desolate valley, where the Jub-Jub bird screams in passion overhead, and the creatures from *The Temptation of St. Anthony* surround them, escape from the destructive power of sex sublimating it into arithmetical calculations based on the number 3.

And Melville, despite his love of physical beauty, in nature and in man, of

> our Pantheistic ports:
> Marquesas and glenned isles that be
> Authentic Edens in a Pagan sea.

can also note in revulsion:

> Found a family, build a state,
> The pledged event is still the same:
> Matter in end will never abate
> His ancient brutal claim.

Baudelaire's ideal man, the Dandy, is, from the point of view of the bourgeois, a wild figure who indulges in every kind of excess, but, from his own, he is a fastidious ascetic who despises the bourgeois because they are "natural."

"Woman is the opposite of the Dandy. Therefore she should inspire horror. Woman is hungry and she wants to eat, thirsty and she wants to drink. She is in rut and she wants to be possessed. Woman is *natural*, that is to say, abominable.

"The Dandy should aspire to be uninterruptedly sublime. He should live and sleep in front of a mirror.

"The more a man cultivates the arts, the less he fornicates.

A more and more apparent cleavage occurs between the spirit and the brute."

(Mon Cœur Mis à Nu)

The Euclidean stone, the transcendent stable reality desired as a haven for the storm-tossed mariner, is not, however, the Transcendental Newtonian God but rather the Platonic Ideas. Geometry does not judge or interfere but is beyond good and evil; it demands nothing but what the mind cares to give it; moreover, it cannot be made use of, it is not one of those ignoble social snarks, you cannot fetch it home and serve it with greens: it is not for striking a light, it is simply itself, and to be oneself is the aim of every romantic.

When Peer Gynt visits the land of the Trolls, the king puts him through a catechism:

K. What is the difference between Trolls and Men?
P. There isn't any, as far as I can gather;
    Big trolls would roast and little ones would claw you—
    Just as with us if only we dared do it.
K. True; we're alike in that and other things too.
    Still, just as morning's different from evening,
    So there's a real difference between us,
    And I will tell you what it is. Out yonder
    Under the skies men have a common saying:
    "Man, to thyself be true!" But here, 'mongst Trolls
    "Troll, to thyself be—enough."

(Peer Gynt II. 6)

To be enough to oneself means to have no conscious ego standing over against the self, to be unable to say no to

oneself, or to distinguish fantasy from reality, not to
be able to lie, to have no name and answer to Hi or to
any loud cry. The siren voice of the poetic shell calls
men to the sea, the double kingdom, to put off their
human nature and be Trolls. The prospect is as alluring
to every man as it was to Faust:

> *Hier fass ich Fuss! Hier sind es Wirklichkeiten,*
> *Von hier aus darf der Geist mit Geistern streiten,*
> *Das Doppelreich, das grosse, sich bereiten.*
> *So fern sie war, wie kann sie näher sein!*
> *Ich rette sie und sie ist doppelt mein.*
>
> (Faust. Part II. I. 5)

yet every man makes his reservations like Peer Gynt.

> I've taken a tail, it is true; but then
> I can undo the knots that our friend has tied,
> And take the thing off. I have shed my breeches;
> They were old and patched; but that won't prevent me
> From putting them on if I have a mind to.
> I shall probably find it just as easy
> To deal with your Trollish way of living.
> I can easily swear that a cow's a maiden;
> An oath's not a difficult thing to swallow.
> But to know that one never can get one's freedom—
> Not even to die as a human being—
> To end one's day as a Troll of the mountains—
> Never go back, as you tell me plainly—
> That is a thing that I'll not submit to.
>
> (Peer Gynt II. 6)

For to submit would be to be swallowed up in the waters, to be drowned in the deluge.

On the other side, the Euclidean stone speaks of a world of pure truth, the image to the weary mariner of all that is true to itself. It is, however, not truth which is enough to itself, and no man can be as a triangle any more than he can be as a troll, for he would have to lose his self and become a purely self-conscious ego whose motto would be "I to I be enough." This is the dilemma of the romantic hero.

THREE

Ishmael—Don Quixote

wwwwwww

"Mes soeurs, n'aimez pas les marins:
La solitude est leur royaume."

JEAN COCTEAU

WHAT IS A HERO? THE EXCEPTIONAL INDIVIDUAL. HOW is he recognised, whether in life or in books? By the degree of interest he arouses in the spectator or the reader. A comparative study, therefore, of the kinds of individuals which writers in various periods have chosen for their heroes often provides a useful clue to the attitudes and preoccupations of each age, for a man's interest always centres, consciously or unconsciously, round what seems to him the most important and still unsolved problem. The hero and his story are simultaneously a stating and a solving of the problem.

HEROIC AUTHORITY

The exceptional individual is one who possesses authority over the average. This authority can be of three kinds, aesthetic, ethical and religious.

AESTHETIC AUTHORITY

Aesthetic authority arises from a necessary inequality of finite individuals in relation to one another. The aesthetic hero is the man to whom fortune has granted exceptional gifts. These may be within himself, e.g., A is more beautiful or cleverer than B, or in the situation in which he is placed, e.g., A is a king, B is a slave.

The inequality is necessary in the first case because beauty or brains are given qualities which cannot be produced or exchanged by any voluntary decision on either side, and in the second because, at any given moment of time in the situation, authority is given to the one.

Since, by virtue of his superior gifts, the hero can do what the average cannot do for themselves, he must do precisely that to be recognised by them as a hero. Thus, if victory over their enemies is what they most desire, he must lead them in war; if victory over nature, he must construct bridges, drain swamps, etc. In return they must give him admiration and obedience. The natural threat to the aesthetic hero is the passing of time, culminating in the inevitable fact of death, which brings him to the same level of nullity as everyone else.

There are also dangers within himself and within the others. For him the danger is pride, i.e., thinking that his superior qualities are not given him by the gods or fate or nature, but earned by him, i.e., that he is not merely luckier than others but intrinsically morally better. If he yields to this, he becomes a tyrant who demands admiration in excess and is insolent towards the powers that gave him his power. Vice versa, the danger for the average is envy, i.e., denying that the inequality is necessary, and wishing to take the hero's place or, if that is impossible, at least to bring him down to their level.

The aesthetic hero is naturally thought of as being happy, for all desire to be as he. He only becomes unhappy when he ceases to be superior, i.e., when he dies, or suffers some great misfortune.

The Homeric kind of hero is pathetic, i.e., his death happens to him without any fault on his part. The hero of Greek drama is tragic because his death is due to pride on his part, and envy on the part of the gods.

ETHICAL AUTHORITY

Ethical authority arises from an accidental inequality in the relation of individuals to the universal truth. The ethical hero is the one who at any given moment happens to know more than the others. This knowledge can be any part of the truth, not only what is commonly called ethics.

E.g. A is ethically superior in relation to B if he knows the multiplication table up to 11 when B only knows it up to 10, just as C is to D, if C knows that it is wrong to steal and D does not yet know it.

Here it is not a question of innate gifts (if A is cleverer than B he is aesthetically superior) but a remediable accident of time and opportunity, i.e., the hero is not one who *can* do what the others cannot, but one who *does* know now what the others *do* not but can be taught by him, which is precisely what he must do if he is to be recognised by them as a hero. In return they give him their attention, as a bridge between them and the truth, for what is required of both is exactly the same, to love and to learn as much about the truth as possible. It is quite possible, for instance, that if A teaches B the eleven times table, so making them equal, B now learns the twelves table before A, and their positions are reversed. It is now B who is the hero.

Here again there are dangers both from without and within. "Without," however, now has a special sense, it means outside the mind, i.e., not from time or fate, but from matter, the needs and passions of the body which interfere with love and study of the truth.

The inner danger is the same for both hero-teacher and inferior pupil, namely, that they will both attempt to treat the situation as an aesthetic relation between them and forget or deny their relations to the truth, which is the important thing. Thus the ethical hero, desiring aesthetic admiration, is tempted to refuse to surrender his superiority and refuse to share his knowledge, treating it instead as a hermetic mystery, the consequence of which is that, thinking always of his relation to the ignorant, he ceases to think about the truth. The inferior, desiring ease and bodily pleasure, are tempted either to refuse to learn from the hero or to adopt a passive attitude of admiration which takes what he says because he says, and not because they can see for themselves that it is the truth.

The Ethical Hero, e.g., Socrates, is thought of as one who is happier than his inferiors because he is already in the movement away from the dark misery of ignorance and servitude to passion towards the bright joy of freedom in knowledge of the truth. Time is not the ultimately overwhelming enemy, but the temporary element through which men move towards immortality.

RELIGIOUS AUTHORITY

Religious authority is like aesthetic authority in that it is not transferable from one individual to another and like ethical authority in that it arises, not from a relation between individuals, but from a relation to truth. But the religious definition of truth is not that it is universal but that it is absolute. The religious hero is one who is committed to anything with absolute passion, i.e., to him it is the absolute truth, his god. The stress is so strongly on the absolute that though he may be passionately related to what, ethically, i.e., universally, is false, he is a religious hero and has religious authority over the one who is lukewarmly or dispassionately related to what is true. Thus, the distinction between being absolutely committed to the real truth, and being absolutely committed to falsehood, is not between being a religious man or not being one, but between the sane and the mad.

In a sense, the religious hero is not related to others at all: his authority cannot command admiration, or transfer knowledge, it can only enkindle by example a similar absolute passion, not necessarily for the same god. (E.g., one has sometimes observed in education that a teacher with a passion for, say, mathematics, has aroused in an unmathematical pupil a passion for, say, Latin.)

The dangers for the religious hero are two: firstly, that he may lose his faith, and so cease to be absolutely committed, and secondly and much more seriously that while continuing to recognise the absolute commitment he should transmute its nature from positive to negative, so that he is committed to the truth in an absolute passion of aversion and hatred. In the first case, he simply ceases to be a religious hero; in the second, he becomes the negative religious hero, i.e., the devil, the absolute villain, Iago or Claggart. The temptation to either arises from expecting something in return for his commitment, i.e., the aesthetic hero may expect happiness so long as he possesses his gifts, but it is his happiness that is a temptation to pride, the ethical hero can look forward to more and more true happiness so long as he perseveres, but it is the pleasures of the body that tempt him to give up his quest, but the religious hero cannot demand happiness, except the happiness of the commitment itself, of love for love's sake. It does not follow that he must necessarily expect misery though, since few desire misery, it is usually misery and not happiness or pleasure that are his temptation; it is more correct to say that whatever he does not expect is temptation.

THE ROMANTIC HERO

In Wordsworth's dream, the hero is described as a combination of a Bedouin desert dweller and Don Quixote; his intention is to carry away symbols of imagination and abstract reason to hide them from the destructive deluge to come; his motive, to save them for future descendants of men, for the age after the Flood. His end is left in doubt, but it seems probable that it is tragic, that he is overwhelmed and fails to save the treasures entrusted to him. Why a Bedouin and why Don Quixote?

ISHMAEL

The Biblical story of the first Bedouin, Ishmael, is given in *Genesis* (chapters XVI and XVII, and chapter XXI). Abraham's wife Sarah is barren, so at her suggestion Abraham lies with a bond-maiden, Hagar. Sarah now becomes jealous and with Abraham's consent treats the pregnant Hagar so badly that she runs away into the desert. But there an angel speaks to her and tells her to return to her mistress, and prophesies:

Behold, thou shalt bear a son, and shalt call his name Ishmael. He will be a wild man; his hand will be against every man, and every man's hand against him: and he shall dwell in the midst of all his brethren.

God also speaks to Abraham:

Sarah thy wife shall bear thee a son indeed and thou shalt call his name Isaac . . . As for Ishmael . . . Behold, I have

blessed him, and will make him a great nation. But my cove-
nant shall be with Isaac which Sarah shall bear unto thee at
this set time in the next year.

In due order first Ishmael and then Isaac are born, but
Sarah is still jealous—in fairness to her she has both
before and now caught Hagar mocking at her—and says
to Abraham:

"Cast out this bondwoman and her son; for the son of this
bondwoman shall not be heir with my son, even with Isaac."
And the thing was very grievous in Abraham's sight because
of his son. And God said unto Abraham, Let it not be grievous
in thy sight because of the lad, and because of thy bondwoman; in all that Sarah hath said unto thee, hearken unto
her voice; for in Isaac shall thy seed be called.
And also of the son of the bondwoman will I make a nation,
because he is thy seed.

Abraham accordingly gives Hagar and Ishmael some
bread and water and turns them out into the desert
where they are about to die of thirst, when God shows
her a well and tells her too that he will make a great
nation of Ishmael.

And God was with the lad; and he grew, and dwelt in the
wilderness, and became an archer.

Translating this story into terms of personality, we get
someone who
1) Is conscious of superior powers. (The first-born)
2) Has a grievance, feeling that he is the victim of some
   wrong for which he is not responsible. (Illegitimate)

3) Does not like and is not liked by the respectable, fashionable and successful of this world (Sarah and Isaac). He despises them for not being gifted as he (Hagar's mocking of Sarah) and they envy and persecute him for the same reason. (Sarah's behaviour towards Hagar)

4) In consequence he is socially an outcast and not easily employable. If he does fall in love, it is an unhappy love. (He dwells in the wilderness)

5) He prefers to spend his time with other social outcasts like himself, with crooks, whores, impressed sailors, etc., of whom there are a good many. (A great nation)

6) In solitude and low company he develops the qualities of courage and tough endurance. (An archer)

7) He is unhappy and lonely, yet cherishes his unhappiness and loneliness as a proof of his superiority. (He chooses to live in the desert)

DON QUIXOTE

When we are first introduced to Don Quixote he is

1) poor

2) not a knight but only the plain Alonso Quixano

3) has had a sort of inclination for a good country lass, though 'tis believed she never heard of it

4) has nothing to do except hunt and read romances about Knight Errantry

5) is slightly mad, i.e., he sells land to buy these books. Suddenly he goes really mad: i.e., instead of being

content to project himself in imagination into the heroes of the books, he sets out to become in reality what he admires and rides off to restore to the fallen world the golden age of chivalry, and to challenge all comers to admit that the obscure country girl is the Princess Dulcinea del Toboso, the most beautiful woman in the world. Naturally enough, he fails in everything. When he thinks he is attacking giants, heretics and heathens he is not only worsted in combat, but attacks innocent people and destroys other people's property.

Further, his madness has two aspects: firstly, the nature of his resolution and secondly the moments in which he sees people and objects as other than they are. The first is constant, the second intermittent. Yet when his vision is sane, i.e., when he sees that the windmills are windmills and not giants, it does not change his original conviction, for he takes his moments of sane vision to be mad and says, "These cursed magicians delude me, first drawing me into dangerous adventures by the appearances of things as they really are and then presently changing the face of things as they please." Even when they meet a plain country wench, whom Don Quixote correctly sees as such, and Sancho Panza for a joke describes her as his ideal lady, the Princess Dulcinea, he believes Sancho Panza against the evidence of his own feelings.

Finally, after many adventures, all of them unsuc-